Riding for the Brand

The Power of Purposeful Leadership

Riding for the Brand
The Power of Purposeful Leadership
By Jim Whitt
Copyright ©2005

ISBN 0-9770004-0-0

Published by Lariat Press
www.lariatpress.com
1-800-874-4928

Foreword

I was sitting in my office in downtown Tulsa when the phone rang. A pleasant voice with an easy Oklahoma drawl introduced himself as Jim Whitt. You could hear his smile through the phone.

He explained he was driving down the road listening to the radio when he heard this guy being interviewed about *The American*, a 21-story bronze statue of a Native American brave, arm raised to receive an American Bald Eagle in flight. The inspiration of sculptor Shan Gray, *The American* is planned to sit atop Holmes Peak in Osage County just northwest of Tulsa.

As it turns out the guy on the radio was me. During the interview I explained the project might be in danger of a funding shortfall and that Tulsa-based financial support was essential if the area was to benefit from the significant economic impact envisioned by the largest private venture of its type ever attempted.

After hearing the interview on the radio Jim called me. He explained he was writing a book that took place 25 years into the future and *The American* played a part in the story line. So he was more than just a little bit concerned when he heard me say that the project might not get off the ground!

We talked only a few minutes before I knew we were kindred spirits. Jim asked if I would mind reading his manuscript. I agreed and life would never be the same. Reading the manuscript was like Bill Murray's experiences in *Groundhog Day*. The setting, the characters, the storyline and the mention of *The American*, all were eerily aligned with both my current experience with the monument and of my life overall. I knew these people, I knew this author and I knew the storyline by heart. Heck, I was living it! So reading the manuscript was fun, validating and a little spooky all at the same time.

I liked Jim from the moment I first laid eyes on him. It would be hard not to like him. He has a glint in his eye that says he is comfortable in his own skin. Ramrod straight with neat, short-cropped hair and a quick, easy smile, Jim has a way of putting people at ease in short order. And it takes no time at all for him to get you into a conversation about his passion... *purpose.*

From the moment I first shook Jim's hand I knew we shared a common purpose, would be partners-for-life, were likely to do some pioneering together and that both our lives and the world would profit from the experience. Since that time, Jim and I have spent many hours sharing our experiences, beliefs and lessons learned in this life. We are sort of like two kids who have discovered that all the chocolate bars in the world have been sitting in our basement all along!

Since *The American* was the catalyst that put our paths on a collision course, we decided to join forces to give everyone a chance to be a part of what will be one of America's greatest monuments. *The American* will be the largest free-standing bronze sculpture in the world and it will stand in the heart of America's heartland. It will be as much a part of the American landscape as *The Statue of Liberty* and *Mount Rushmore*. You can learn more about *The American* at www.ridingforthebrand.com. Jim has graciously committed a portion of the proceeds from this book towards the funding of *The American*. So with the purchase of this book you became our partner in this project.

This book is much more than a good read with an interesting story, though it is certainly that, at the very least. In its pages you'll discover how people and organizations can be transformed by the power of purpose. The principles of purposeful leadership can be applied to any organization including small businesses, corporations, nonprofits, associations and governments. The lessons you'll learn can be applied to cities, states and countries. If you want to live and lead *on purpose* then saddle up — you're ready to ride for the brand.

Bob Workman

May 2005

In addition to serving as the Tulsa spokesperson for The American project, Bob Workman is cofounder and chairman of BSW International, Inc. which has provided design and architectural services for nearly 8,000 building projects worldwide including 4,000 Wal-Mart Stores and Sam's Wholesale Clubs. He is also cofounder and president of BOX Master Builders, Inc., cofounder and president of SOL, Inc. and cofounder and director of Lucernex, Inc.

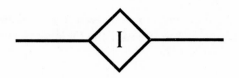

"**S**ing for me, Grandpa."

"What do you want to hear, boy?"

"You know," Bobby said excitedly.

"San Antonio Rose?"

"No!"

"Faded Love?"

"No, you know... *Oklahoma Hills!*"

The old man scratched his head, "I don't know if I can remember the words."

"Come on, Grandpa, don't tease!"

"Well, let's see..."

The boy watched anxiously as his grandpa picked up a well-worn guitar that was leaning against the wall. He cradled it in his lap, tuned it a little and then broke into song.

> *'Way down yonder in the Indian nation*
> *I rode my pony on the reservation*
> *In the Oklahoma Hills where I was born*
> *'Way down yonder in the Indian nation*
> *A cowboy's life is my occupation*
> *In the Oklahoma Hills where I born*

The youngster never tired of his grandpa's singing but as the night wore on, his eyelids grew heavy and he drifted into the place of his dreams — a place where time stood still and cowboys and Indians forever rode the Oklahoma Hills. And he was right there with them...

Bobby felt a tap on his shoulder. It must be morning but he felt like he really hadn't slept at all.

"Grandpa?"

He blinked but Grandpa was nowhere in sight. Instead he found himself staring into the eyes of a very bemused flight attendant.

"I'm not your grandpa, sir."

Bob rubbed his eyes. "Oh, sorry... I must have dropped off for a minute."

"Sir, we're making our descent. You'll need to buckle your seatbelt and bring your seatback forward."

It had been a long time since Bob had been home. He never dreamed he would land an assignment that would take him back to Oklahoma. But his dream had already brought him back. He smiled. He could still hear his grandpa singing...

Many months have come and gone
Since I wandered from my home
In those Oklahoma Hills where I was born

As the plane banked for the approach, Bob looked out the window and was temporarily blinded by the early morning sun as it reflected off the buildings that formed the skyline of downtown Tulsa. Tulsa was just a sleepy cow town until Robert F. Galbreath and Frank Chesley noticed oil stains on a limestone formation while camping out on Robert and Ida Glenn's farm south of town in 1905. Galbreath took a sledgehammer to the rock and oil literally oozed from the limestone. It wasn't long after that the *Glenn Pool* field was producing more oil than the entire state of Texas. It was one of many such Oklahoma oil fields that would make Tulsa the undisputed *Oil Capital of the World.*

The oil boom was on but cattle still grazed the Oklahoma Hills. Oil and agriculture were the two sides of the business coin in 20th century Oklahoma. In nearby Osage County, where Bob was born and raised, most people's livelihoods were tied to one or both of these two industries. It was just like Grandpa's song.

> *Now as I turn life a page*
> *To the land of the great Osage*
> *Where the black oil rolls and flows*
> *And the snow-white cotton grows*

It was the legendary Woody Guthrie and his brother Jack who put those words to song. *Oklahoma Hills* was an anthem to the state they came of age in. Woody described his home town of Okemah as, "...one of the singingest, square dancingest, drinkingest, yellingest, preachingest, walkingest, talkingest, laughingest, cryingest, shootingest, fist fightingest, bleedingest, gamblingest, gun, club and razor carryingest of our ranch towns and farm towns, because it blossomed out into one of our first oil boom towns." That was before the drought stricken years of the 1930s scorched the amber waves of grain on America's fruited plains. The Dust Bowl needed a face and Oklahoma became the reluctant model for unflattering portraits by photographers, artists and writers. When John Steinbeck wrote about the fictional Jode family in *The Grapes of Wrath*, Oklahomans simply became known as *Okies*.

The Dirty Thirties came and went but the soil and oil of the Oklahoma Hills endured. Rodgers and Hammerstein gave the state a much needed face lift in 1943 when their musical *Oklahoma!* broke all Broadway box office records. The lyrics of the memorable title song restored the image of Oklahoma to its former glory:

We know we belong to the land
And the land we belong to is grand!

By 1969 Merle Haggard was even "proud to be an Okie from Muskogee." But by the end of the 20th century most of the oil companies had relocated their headquarters to Houston, the international hub of the energy business. Oil barons no longer came to Tulsa to broker deals but millions of people flocked to Tulsa each year to see the world's largest freestanding bronze sculpture, *The American*. Shan Gray's twenty-one story statue of an Indian warrior with an eagle perched on his outstretched arm was awe inspiring.

"The Statue of Liberty should be jealous," Bob thought as he drove past in his rental car. It was good to be back in the hills of Oklahoma and the giant warrior seemed to be welcoming Bob home.

Bob had grown up on a ranch but it had been many years since the cowboy's life had been *his* occupation. *Cowboys and Indians* pretty much described Oklahoma before the discovery of oil catapulted the territory into statehood in 1907. Fate had smiled upon the Osage tribe — they retained all of the mineral rights in the Osage Nation. Unlike many of their brethren who lived in poverty on reservations scattered across North America, the Osages weren't poor. Oil coursed through the limestone veins underneath the Oklahoma Hills and if Osage blood coursed through your veins you shared in the wealth. That wealth was commonly reinvested into land and cattle. Indians still rode the hills but the oil boom elevated their standard of living. They could drive a Cadillac instead of going horseback.

Cadillacs, and most other motor vehicles, were now hydrogen powered. PHCs (personal hover craft) were becoming affordable and a sizable number of the public owned them. The power lines that followed the highways were becoming scarce now that *fuel cells* had become the energy source of choice by more homes and businesses. Once the air traffic control problem was resolved and PHCs were no longer restricted by law to follow roads, Bob wondered if cars with wheels would end up as museum pieces. Transportation infrastructure could be transformed from concrete and asphalt into *virtual* highways. High-speed bullet trains were carrying more people and goods across the nation. *Teleportation* was proving to be more than just a figment of H.G. Wells's imagination. It wasn't too many years ago that it seemed crazy to think that matter actually could be dematerialized at one point and recreated at another. But ongoing research was starting to show that maybe Scotty really could beam up Captain Kirk.

Bob sometimes thought about what it would be like to travel back in time. As he drove, he imagined what the landscape might look like if the millions of acres of highway right-of-way could be returned to their native state. *Native State* was an accurate description of Oklahoma. The name comes from two Choctaw words: "okla" meaning people, and "humma" meaning red. Oklahoma was still the land of the red people. The Osage and Choctaw were among thirty-nine Native American tribes headquartered there — more than any other state.

Bob aimed his car north on Highway 75 in the direction of Bartlesville, the birthplace of Phillips Petroleum. Frank Phillips, a barber from Iowa, had come to Oklahoma in 1903 prospecting for black gold and hit the mother lode. It was the famous Burbank oilfield that made *Uncle Frank* — as he was known to his employees and the people of Bartlesville — a multimillionaire. Uncle Frank went on to that great oilfield in the sky in 1950 but his company carried on until 2003, when it merged with Conoco. Based in Ponca City, Conoco was formed when Marland Oil merged with the Continental Oil Company in 1928. Like Frank Phillips, E.W. Marland owed much of his fortune to the Burbank Field. After the merger, ConocoPhillips joined the energy exodus across the Red River and moved their headquarters to Houston. This move that involved what used to be the two crown jewels of the Oklahoma oil industry unofficially marked the closing of a glorious era. The *Oil Capital* mantle that Tulsa had so proudly worn for so many years was unceremoniously passed on to its Texas cousin.

Bob turned westward on Highway 11. This stretch of highway snakes through blackjack covered hills interrupted frequently by vast expanses of pastureland. As the Guthries' song so eloquently put it:

> *Where the oak and blackjack trees*
> *Kiss the playful prairie breeze*

The blackjacks thinned out as Bob continued west of Pawhuska, the Osage County seat, on Highway 60. He was now in the *Tallgrass Prairie* — cow country as it used to be called. Bob's destination was Field's Corner, a point on the map located roughly halfway between the forty-two miles that separated Pawhuska and Ponca City. To the locals the Burbank oilfield had simply been known as *The Field*. Field's Corner earned its name because it was situated on the corner of that field. The high water mark for The Field was in 1923 when it covered more than 20,000 acres and produced more than 32 million barrels of crude. By the end of the 1990s the massive Lufkin pump jacks that once dotted the landscape to suck the oil from the ground had just about disappeared.

Now, the once legendary Burbank Field was merely a footnote in the oil-rich history of Oklahoma. Some of the 20th century's great success stories were birthed in that field. Now, it was agriculture, the other side of the Oklahoma business coin that would make it home to one of the great success stories of the 21st Century.

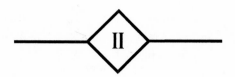

II

The year was 2030 and agriculture had evolved into a highly technical and sophisticated food chain. And that's what brought Bob back to Osage County. The onetime cowboy was now a freelance writer. When he was punching cows as a youngster he would have laughed out loud if someone had told him he'd be making a living as a wordsmith. It didn't seem real. Here he was back in his old stomping grounds to write a story. He felt like a character in a science fiction movie caught in some kind of time warp. One day he's horseback turning a cow and poof, he reappears with a word processor turning a phrase.

A large overarching gate marked the entrance to the subject of his assignment. It was constructed from massive limestone pillars. A wooden sign spanned the top of the pillars. A diamond shaped brand had been burned into the center of the sign sandwiched between the words Diamond Enterprises. Bob drove across the welded pipe *cattle guard* that bridged the pillars onto an asphalt road that wound through a pasture where cattle grazed. On the other side of a low-water bridge spanning a small creek, a large ranch style building came into view. It too, was constructed of limestone rock and cedar. Bob smiled. You didn't have to look far to find limestone in the Osage. It pushed up through the earth's surface and spilled out like broken strings of craggy gray pearls tucked between the purple-hued clumps of native bluestem grass.

Not far under the rich topsoil, the limestone formed solid sheets of bedrock, like those where Robert Galbreath unleashed the flow of oil that became the Glenn Pool. Bob knew all about limestone. He had built plenty of fence growing up, and digging postholes in the rocky soil was a challenge. Instead of setting conventional corner posts, his dad had taught him how to make *rock corners*. Making a four-foot diameter cylinder from hog wire, Bob filled the cylinder with pieces of limestone stacking them to a height of about five feet. He could always find enough rock within a short distance to fill the cylinder. Once a common sight in the area, the rock corners looked like miniature monuments scattered across the prairie connecting the barbed wire fences.

Bob cooled his heels in the waiting area of the office while the receptionist announced his arrival. The building's interior was simple and rustic. You might say it was decorated in West by Southwest. Navajo rugs were scattered about the hardwood floors and Western art adorned the walls. The receptionist returned shortly with a tall, rugged looking man in tow. His hair was white, his faced was tanned and weathered and his manner was easy. He was up in years but one of those people that you couldn't quite peg on the age chart. He smiled, stuck out his hand and said, "I'm Burns Marcus."

"Bob Fooshee."

Burns Marcus looked Bob up and down — he didn't look like a writer. In fact, he looked like a younger version of Burns Marcus. And like Marcus, he was wearing a pair of starched Wranglers and cowboy boots. "I used to know some Fooshees. Are you from around here?"

"Used to be. I grew up on the Arkansas River over by Ponca."

"I didn't know what a writer was supposed to look like but I wasn't expecting someone who looked like one of our ranch hands. We might put you to work around here if you don't watch out."

Bob laughed. "Well, I guess you can take a cowboy out of the country but you can't take the country out of the cowboy."

"Have a cup of coffee, Bob?"

"That sounds good."

After they stopped off at the break room for coffee the two men headed back to Burns's office and parked in a couple of leather-bound wing chairs.

"I've been looking forward to this assignment, Mr. Marcus."

"Call me Burns. Do you have any family left over by Ponca, Bob?"

"No. Mom and Dad are both gone. And after they passed away we sold the place."

"So now you're a writer. And for the life of me, I can't understand why you want to write about some broken-down old cowboy like me."

"Well, Burns, you can only fly under the radar for so long. Diamond Enterprises isn't exactly a secret anymore."

"I was kind of hoping if we kept our headquarters out here in the middle of nowhere we might go unnoticed. But I have to admit, even though I'm not always fond of the attention it brings, I am proud of what we've accomplished. It's been fun."

Fun. Bob had interviewed a lot of CEOs in his day, but not many talked about their businesses being fun.

"It's been fun?"

"More than I could have ever imagined. But it wasn't always that way. In fact, there was a time when I was just flat out miserable. Grab your coffee and let's go jump in my pickup. I'll show you around and tell you how miserable I used to be."

It's hard to keep a cowboy cooped up in an office. They'll look for most any excuse to escape and Bob was the older man's excuse. They drove and talked.

"I grew up here too, Bob. In fact this was the home place. Went off to college, got a degree in animal science and decided to seek fame and fortune in corporate America. I took a job in sales with a pharmaceutical company. I started out on the animal health side but animal health was falling out of favor with the company because of shrinking profits. So, I switched to the human health side and spent my days calling on hospitals, clinics and medical practices pushing pills to doctors.

"I was good at sales and before long was given the opportunity to go into marketing. That meant moving to the company's headquarters in New Jersey. I liked marketing but sometimes I was just a little too plain spoken to successfully navigate the maze of corporate politics. Life in the 'head shed' was a real eye opener for me. I soon found myself disillusioned with life on the corporate treadmill and started looking for a hole in the fence to jump through. I found a hole but the circumstances that created it were not exactly what I expected — or wanted.

"I got a call from home one day. Dad had suffered a heart attack. To make a long story short, I loaded up the wife and kids and moved back here to take over the family ranch. I got off the corporate treadmill and traded my suit and tie for boots and jeans. That was about 30 years ago."

"Thirty years," Bob mused aloud. "Things were really changing in the cattle business back then, weren't they?"

"I was about to find out just how much they *were* changing. It was all good in the first few years. I felt like a bird that had been let out of a cage. Being back in the country was like a tonic. My wife was happy, the kids were happy and I was happy. Then Dad's heart finally gave out for good. It was my show then and I got a lesson on why the profits were shrinking in animal health when I was in the pharmaceutical business. Profits were shrinking in the livestock business. Agriculture, like all other industries, was consolidating rapidly. If you were a small operator it was a tough row to hoe.

"It looked like the best option was to get bigger to take advantage of economies of scale. So I borrowed more money and expanded the operation. I thought things would get better but they just kept getting worse. I was like the hay hauler who was losing a $1.00 a bale and decided the solution was to buy a bigger truck. He just went broke faster and I did too. Before long, owning this ranch wasn't fun anymore. My wife started teaching school to help make ends meet and I was looking for answers. I was so miserable that my days on the corporate treadmill were starting to look good again.

"Misery loves company and I found plenty of it. There were lots of other farmers and ranchers I knew who were singing the blues too. We were all just trying to figure out how to hang on. But I was losing my grip. I couldn't hang on much longer.

"This was my state of mind when I headed to the annual cattle industry convention. I needed help so I went to the convention in search of answers."

B urns did most of the talking and Bob did most of the listening. Even though the ranch and cattle operations were now a miniscule part of Diamond Enterprises, Bob enjoyed the tour. It was late springtime in the Osage. You could almost see the grass grow. It was a stroll down memory lane for Bob and he would have been content listening to Burns talk about cattle all day but he felt compelled to get back to the story. How did a guy who was going broke three decades ago turn a nearly bankrupt ranch into a business empire?

"What happened at the convention, Burns?"

"The convention? Oh, the convention. Well, as I said I was looking for answers and the cattlemen's convention was in San Antonio. I thought since I was going broke anyway I might as well head to the Alamo for my last stand, so to speak. Why not go out with a bang? So, the wife and I flew to San Antonio. The first morning of the convention she headed for the Riverwalk and I headed to the convention hall.

"I got to the opening general session just in time to find one of the last seats right down in front. The keynote speaker was a guy they introduced as a professional provoker — his bio in the program said he was 'someone who would challenge you to think about what you do, why you do it and how to change it.' That's just what I wanted — or at least what I thought I wanted. I needed to change what I was doing or I was going to go belly up.

"This guy was equal parts management consultant, motivational speaker and standup comic. He started out really good and I was settled in enjoying his talk when he started to provoke *me*."

"What do you mean?"

"It's funny. The thing that provoked me was just a simple question: 'What's *your* purpose in life?'"

"Why did that provoke you?"

"Well, here I was trying to figure out how to survive and he turns pop psychologist on me. That's what provoked me. In fact, it made me mad as hell. I didn't need to 'get in touch with my feelings.' Who'd he think he was — Dr. Phil?"

"Dr. Phil?"

"You know... he was a psychologist who used to be on television way back when. He got his big break on *Oprah*."

Bob just shrugged.

Burns felt old all of a sudden. He wondered how many people even remembered who Oprah and Dr. Phil were.

"Anyway, what kind of a question was that? 'What's my purpose in life?' I didn't need *questions*, I needed answers! What did this have to do with helping me save the ranch? What I really needed was a silver bullet — a solution for all of my problems — but it was obvious to me that this guy wasn't the Lone Ranger. He didn't have any silver bullets. So, I folded my arms, slumped down in my seat and tuned him out. I would have walked out if I hadn't been stuck in the middle of the front row. But as soon as he was through I stormed out of the meeting room, out of the convention hall and just kept walking. Maybe I could catch up with my wife on the Riverwalk. Well, that was like finding a needle in a haystack, so I stopped at a sidewalk café, had a cold beer and started talking to myself.

"After awhile I became bored with the conversation and started walking again. I was so wound up I could have walked all the way back to Oklahoma. Then I thought, what the heck, I'm in San Antonio. Why not relax and enjoy it? So, I sauntered down the Riverwalk and my blood pressure started subsiding. I was feeling pretty good again and wandered into a bookstore. I thought I might find a good book that would take my mind off my troubles. *Then it happened...*

"Say, Bob, are you about ready for lunch?"

"Lunch? You can't leave me hanging like that, Burns! What happened?"

"Oh, come on. We gotta eat. Let's go up to the house and see what's cookin'."

Burns took off on a gravel road that led farther up into the pasture and ended up on a plateau with a breathtaking view of the valley below. "Dad," Burns said, gesturing with a sweep of his hand, "used to call this the high-and-wide."

That, Bob thought, *was a perfect description.* Below them was a vast sea of grass filled with bluestem waves driven by a gentle breeze. The valley was split undecidedly by Salt Creek which meandered along nature's time honored path of least resistance. "When I was a kid I tried to imagine what it would be like to have been here when Oklahoma was first being settled."

Burns nodded his head knowingly. "My grandpa told me that when he was a boy the grass was so tall that he couldn't see the cows. He said he could ride his horse all the way to the Kansas state line and never get off to open a gate."

Bob imagined that Burns's wife would have lunch ready for them. He smiled to think that he was so old-fashioned — not to mention hopelessly politically incorrect — as to expect a woman to be waiting inside, ready with a meal for the men folk. That's how it once was when times were simpler. But his vision of yesteryear was obliterated the minute they stepped up on the porch and the door flew open. Out came a woman from the *inside* who was obviously in a big hurry to be on the *outside*.

"Where's the fire?" Burns asked.

"Gotta run," she answered as she breezed by.

"Wait a minute. I want to introduce you to Bob Fooshee, the writer I told you about."

"Oh, I'm sorry. Hi Bob. I'm Jane Marcus. I can't stay. I'm running late. Catch up with you all later." And with that she bounded off the porch, into her car and left in a cloud of dust, leaving the men staring in her wake.

"I can't keep up with that woman," Burns said as he shook his head and ushered Bob through the still-open door. The house was built in the same style as the office — rustic limestone and cedar. Burns led them into the kitchen, opened the refrigerator, pulled out a couple of vacuum sealed plastic envelopes, popped them into the Zip Oven and less than a minute later the two men were sitting down to a meal that would have made a chef jealous.

"This is one of our Zip-N-Eat meals, Bob."

Bob was familiar with Diamond's products with the distinctive diamond shaped brand "burned" into the label. Toss in their development of the Zip Oven and it was not an exaggeration to say that Diamond had changed the way people eat.

"As my wife just so vividly demonstrated, Bob, we live in the same fast-paced world as everybody else. Zip technology is great isn't it? It's like a microwave on steroids. A hot meal in seconds. Time is precious. One of the things I'm most proud of is that we've given people a way to enjoy great meals with virtually no time in preparation. I like to think we've helped put families back around the dinner table — where they can spend a little time together."

Microwaves — the technology of yesteryear that seemed so revolutionary at the time — was now hopelessly outdated. What people used to expect in minutes they could now have in seconds. And they continued to expect things to be faster and better. Did technology have to keep pace with people or did people have to keep pace with technology? It seemed to Bob that the answer was *yes*. Bob's thoughts turned quickly back to their conversation that had been so abruptly interrupted by Burns's hunger pangs back in the pasture.

"What happened?" Bob asked.

"Happened?" Burns looked puzzled.

"In the bookstore. You know... the bookstore... on the Riverwalk in San Antonio. You said, 'Then it happened.'"

"Oh, the bookstore. As I was saying, I had just about regained my composure and was breathing normally again when I looked down and saw a book with the word *purpose* in the title. And guess who the author was? That *yahoo* I just heard speak at the convention — you know, the *professional provoker.* It didn't seem like I could shake this guy. I picked the book up and was thumbing through the pages, when my eye locked onto this sentence on one of the pages: 'What's *your* purpose in life?' I began to wonder if *somebody* wasn't trying to tell me something — or I guess it would be more accurate to say trying to *ask* me something. I was looking for an *answer* and all I was finding was a *question*. Anyway, now that I was clothed and in my right mind, I thought maybe I could find the *answer* in his book."

"So you bought it."

"Yep. Not only that, I started reading it. In fact, I couldn't put it down," Burns said as he stood up, walked over to the kitchen counter, and picked up a well-worn book.

"Did you find the *answer* you were looking for in the book?"

Burns smiled and shook his head. "No. *I found out I already had the answer*. The book just helped me find it.

"You know what's interesting? This all took place in San Antonio. I got to thinking. When every man was lost in the battle at the Alamo it seemed to be the beginning of the end. But it was really just the beginning. You might say Texas was birthed at the Alamo.

"I was at the end of my rope when I went to San Antonio. But what seemed to be the beginning of the end for me was really just the beginning. You could say Diamond Enterprises was birthed there. It all started with *that* question, 'What's your purpose in life?'"

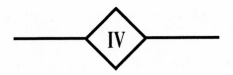

Bob had interviewed a lot of interesting people. He started out writing for a news service but became quickly bored with "just the facts" journalism. It was people's stories that fascinated him. It didn't make any difference to him whether the subject was a celebrity, a business person or a prison inmate. His assignments had taken him to Wall Street, death row and Hollywood — and that was before the entertainment industry left Hollywood for Texas. It seemed like everybody had moved to Texas.

Bob believed everyone had a story to tell and that everyone's story was significant. It must have been the cowboy in him — cowboys used to pass the time around a campfire swapping stories. And Bob was a storyteller at heart.

Over the years Bob had learned that researching a story was a lot like peeling an onion. Burns's search for an answer to a simple question twenty-five years ago was like another layer of the onion. It was a story within the story.

"As I read this book," Burns said as he handed it to Bob, "I started finding my life's story in its pages. There was an exercise at the end of each chapter that made me reflect on different experiences and times in my life — the good, the bad and yes, even the ugly.

"The process was like collecting clues in a scavenger hunt designed to help me find my purpose. It forced me to review my whole life from the perspective of why I was put here on planet earth. It made me analyze the impact my life has on the lives of others.

"And you know what's funny? As I read the book, I could see a lot of similarities between the life of the author — the *professional provoker* — and my life. He had been searching for answers just like I was — and that's what led him to the discovery of his purpose.

"If you think about it, it's human nature to question why we're here. Not just in the general sense, but each individual intuitively believes there has to be a reason for *his* or *her* existence."

"So, did you find *your* purpose?"

"Not right away. I started reading the book on the flight back to Tulsa and wrote out my answers to all the questions. By the time I was finished I had a mini-autobiography. It was like weaving a tapestry of my life's story but the picture was camouflaged into the fabric. I couldn't quite figure out the pattern. It was just a blur of disconnected shapes and colors.

"For the next week I couldn't stop thinking about it. I ruminated on it — rereading the book and my answers to the questions. It seemed like each day I took a step back and the picture became clearer until one day it all came into focus. *I knew what my purpose was.*"

Bob was beginning to appreciate the fact that Burns was a pretty good storyteller himself. He kept leading him to the edge of the cliff and then left him hanging.

"And…?"

"I realized my purpose is to 'feed a hungry world.' It was a recurring theme throughout my answers. Ever since I was a kid, it bothered me to know that there were people going to bed hungry every night. To this day I still can't stand to see people leave food on their plates. I'm an easy mark for a panhandler. I have to drag them into the nearest eatery and buy them a meal."

Bob was trying to piece all this together in his mind. Burns was about to go broke ranching... then he goes to a convention and some speaker provokes him to wrath... he reads the speaker's book and finds out he's supposed to "feed the world".... this just wasn't making a lot of sense.

"You're not much of poker player, Bob. You look like a cow standin' at a new gate. I've got you completely bumfuzzled don't I?"

"I'm just trying to connect all the dots," Bob said, embarrassed that his expression had given him away. "Maybe I'm getting ahead of myself... trying to figure out what all this has got to do with Diamond Enterprises."

"That's OK, Bob, when I found my purpose I didn't understand it either. I had no idea the impact that discovery would have on my life. It not only transformed my life, it was the *catalyst* that launched Diamond Enterprises.

"Have you ever thought how much of our lives revolve around eating? Eating is not just a matter of sustenance. The dinner table is where friends and families congregate and celebrate. Life's rites of passage — births, birthdays, marrying and burying — all bring people to a table for a meal. When we get a promotion or bring in that big account we wine and dine to mark the occasion.

"The Bible says God owns the cattle on a thousand hills. A lot of 'em are right here in these Oklahoma Hills. I figured he entrusted their care to me. Most of what I've done in my life has revolved around the business of producing food. I was born and raised in the middle of the world's breadbasket — the heart of the most prolific food-producing nation in the world. It seemed to me all of this didn't happen by chance."

Bob was half expecting Burns to be transfigured into a white-bearded cowboy icon bearing stone tablets with his purpose inscribed on them. Was this guy for real?

Burns smiled sheepishly and sat back down, "Sorry, I can get pretty wound up sometimes."

There was no transfiguration, no parting of the clouds accompanied by thunder and lightning. But there was no doubt that what Burns described as the discovery of his purpose was a significant event in his life. The tone of his voice changed when he talked about it. His easy-going cadence quickened to a passionate pitch. The time passed quickly and the conversation at the kitchen table ran late into the afternoon.

"Let's go out and stretch our legs a bit," Burns suggested.

A southwesterly breeze offered the perfect complement to the bright sunshine, making the temperature seem just a shade cooler than it really was. A cloud of dust coming up the drive was preceded by the same vehicle that Jane had disappeared in just before lunch. She stepped out of the car in a manner that said that she didn't possess the same sense of urgency as when she had left.

"Get that fire put out?" Burns asked.

"Fire? Oh, I didn't mean to be rude. You know how I am, Burns. I get my mind locked onto something and I've got to get it done. I don't suppose you boys starved in my absence did you?"

"You know better than that. The best thing about Diamond brand products is even somebody as culinary-challenged as me can cook a real meal. I'm going to run Bob back down to the office so he can get his car and bring it back up to the house. I told you he was spending the night didn't I?"

"No, but since when do you tell me anything?"

"I didn't mean to put you all out," Bob interjected, looking uncomfortable.

"Oh, don't pay any attention to us," she said smiling. "This is just a little game we play. When you get to be our age, Bob, you won't be able to remember half of what you say either. I was expecting you. I just have to keep Burns guessing."

The "boys" as Jane called them, took off for the office.

Steaks — grilled the old fashioned way — were on the evening menu and afterwards, Burns, Jane and Bob retired to the porch and reminisced about the days when oil was still king of the Osage. The perpetual "pop, pop, pop" of the pump jack engines that used to echo through the night had gone silent years ago. But some things hadn't changed. The lonesome howls of coyotes could be heard as daylight turned to dusk.

"Burns, just reading between the lines, I'd guess your purpose of feeding a hungry world ended up being a line in the mission statement of Diamond Enterprises."

"We don't have a mission statement, Bob."

"No mission statement?"

"Nope. When Diamond was no more than just a gleam in my eye and I was putting together some semblance of a business plan, I studied a lot of other businesses' mission statements. I was visiting with my banker one morning and asked if the bank had one. He said indeed they did — the bank examiners *required* it.

"So, I asked him what their mission was. His lips started moving but no words were coming out of his mouth. Completely flustered, he excused himself and returned after a few minutes with an official looking document carrying the title of *Mission Statement*. He looked pretty pleased with himself.

"I read it, then excused myself and spent the next fifteen minutes talking to employees at the bank and asked them to tell me what the mission was."

"And what did they say?"

"They started stammering just like the president did. Oh, they could recite a word or two from here or there but it was pretty hit and miss."

"I'll bet they were embarrassed."

"Not nearly as much as the president when I told him the results of my impromptu survey. That really ticked him off. So, I just turned his mission statement face down on his desk and asked him to tell me what it said. Exasperated he blurted out, 'Everyone in this bank knows what the mission is. It's to kiss the customer's lips until they're chapped!'

"I had to restrain myself from laughing. I wanted to tell him that the customers probably were chapped, but I'll bet it wasn't their lips."

Bob *didn't* restrain *his* laughter. "I'd like to have seen that."

"It was pretty comical. It's funny but none of the bank's employees mentioned anything about *kissing* and *chapped lips* when I asked them what the mission was. When I read it I couldn't find anything like that in there either."

"So, what *did* it say?"

"It was a long diatribe filled with a lot of well-meaning but meaningless verbiage punctuated with this phrase: '...to enhance the shareholders' equity.'"

"But that's what most mission statements look like, Burns. Nobody pays any attention to them anyway."

"That's the whole point. Most mission statements are created for all the wrong reasons. Since they're *meaningless*, they're ignored. But I learned a good lesson that day. If no one in the organization can tell you what the mission is, there is no mission. It's as simple as that. Secondly, profitability is a given if you are a for-profit business. You *have to* make a profit to stay in business. Putting something like that into a mission statement is like saying the sky is blue. And how motivating do you think 'enhancing the shareholders' equity' is to the employees?"

"Not at all. But isn't profit *the reason* a business exists?"

"No. A business exists *to serve* a customer. Profit is a byproduct of successfully serving that customer. If profitability is the reason a business exists, then we all ought to be selling cocaine."

"So you just decided to *not* have a mission statement?"

"That's right — at least not in the traditional sense. I don't want anyone at Diamond to have to go running for a piece of paper if someone asks what our mission is. The words *mission statement* conjure up the image of a document like the banker handed me. We don't use the term *mission* for just that reason. Instead we talk about our *purpose*.

"Our purpose is to feed a hungry world. Ask anybody around here what our purpose is and that's what they'll tell you."

"And that *motivates* them?"

"If it doesn't, they won't work here. You see, when I started putting Diamond Enterprises together, I didn't just hire people, I enlisted *hunger fighters* — people who didn't just want to work for a paycheck but who wanted to be a soldier in a cause — something bigger than themselves."

Bob slumped back in his chair. If he had learned anything in his interviews with truly successful people, he found they often marched to the beat of a different drummer. But this cat Marcus pushed the boundaries of commonly accepted business philosophy into uncharted territory.

"You look bushed, Bob. Why don't we call it a day and we'll get after it again early in the morning."

Bob wasn't going to argue. He was suffering from brain overload. He walked out to his car to get his bag and took one long, last look at the moon that illuminated the valley below. The spring air had turned chilly now. He closed his eyes to savor the moment and felt like he was caught in that time warp again. In his mind's eye, he was transported back to his boyhood. It was an evening like this and he was sitting on the porch listening to Grandpa play his guitar and sing.

Many a page of life has turned
Many a lesson I have learned
Yet I feel like in those hills I still belong

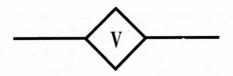

As the sun peeked over the horizon a small covey of quail inched their way across the dew-covered lawn. Bob stood at the kitchen window and watched the show while he sipped his morning coffee.

"How long has it been since you've been horseback, Bob?" Burns asked as he joined him.

"It's been awhile. Why do you ask?"

"Oh, I thought we might ride a little pasture this morning. We could ride and talk. Think you could handle that?"

"I'll be saddle sore tonight but I'm game."

"Good, let's get going. I told our foreman to saddle up a green colt for you — one that had a little buck in him."

Bob smiled but didn't saying anything. He figured Burns was pulling his leg but he also knew from experience that cowboys are notorious practical jokers. He'd been the recipient — and instigator — of many pranks himself in his former life.

He had spent one of his summers between college semesters cowboying in a feedyard in the Texas Panhandle. It was a good sized outfit for back then — 60,000 head of cattle and about twenty cowboys to take care of 'em. Rattlesnakes populated the area and it wasn't unusual to find one curled up in an abandoned prairie dog hole if you were riding in one of the nearby pastures. Leyton, one of the cowboys he worked with was deathly afraid of snakes.

The cowboys all gathered in the break room of the headquarters each day for lunch. One day Bob decided to play a little trick on the rattlesnake-phobic Leyton. He took a paper-clip and opened it up making two "poles" — like a miniature goalpost. He strung a rubber band through a button and attached it to the two poles of the paper clip. Winding the rubber band between the two poles, he carefully inserted the apparatus into an envelope on which he simply inscribed the words *rattlesnake eggs*.

While seated at a table in the break room, Bob presented Leyton with the envelope. Leyton eyed the inscription and nervously opened the envelope. This relieved the pressure of the twisted rubber band. The result was a sound which resembled the *rattle* of the rattlesnake. In one step Leyton leapt from his chair onto the table planting his foot squarely in the middle of Bob's sandwich. In another step he bounded out the break room door, jumped onto his horse which was tied outside and rode off in a dead run while the cowboy crew howled with laughter. It ruined Bob's lunch but it made the cowboy crew's day.

With this memory in mind, Bob thought there was always the possibility that "the writer from the city" was scheduled as the morning's entertainment for the ranch hands. When they pulled up to the barn two geldings were saddled and tied to the corral fence. One was a stout looking buckskin and the other a bay. As they climbed out of the pickup a tall, slender woman with long auburn hair walked out of the barn, untied the horses and led them to Burns and Bob.

"Bob, meet our foreman, Sandy Burton. Sandy this is Bob Fooshee."

Sandy looked like anything *but* a foreman. She could have been one of the models that graced the covers of some of the magazines Bob wrote for — except that she was outfitted in boots and jeans.

Burns nodded towards the buckskin, "I see you saddled up *Widow Maker* for Bob."

"Yes sir," Sandy answered with twinkle in her eye. "You said you wanted to see a rodeo this morning."

Bob knew he was in the clear now. If they had intended to have a little fun at his expense they wouldn't have given him this much warning. And he could tell by looking at the buckskin that he was no green colt. He didn't have to mouth him to know he had a little age on him.

"We're just messin' with you, Bob," Burns said as he swung up on the bay. "Old Buck here is who we put the grandkids on."

Bob adjusted the stirrups and made sure the cinch was good and snug. Even though "old Buck" looked harmless he still wasn't going to take any chances. He climbed into the saddle and kept a tight rein — just in case Buck decided to live up to his name and pitch a little just for old time's sake.

Burns lined the bay out into a lope and Bob followed his lead. It had been a long time since he had been in the saddle. It felt good to have the wind in his face and get in rhythm with the horse. You could cover a lot of ground in a lope and it's an easy gait for both man and horse.

As they topped a hill a five-strand barbed wire fence came into sight. Burns slowed the bay down to a trot, pulled up at a gate and stepped down to open it.

Now, on the other side, the men let their horses walk. Burns reached into his shirt pocket, pulled out a piece of notebook paper folded into fourths and handed it to Bob.

"What's this?"

"After we talked about the purpose of Diamond Enterprises yesterday, I wrote down something I learned from the professional provoker's book. He said there were four elements of purpose as it applies to our lives as individuals. I found that the same four elements could be applied to the purpose of an organization."

Bob unfolded the paper. Burns had drawn a diamond in the middle of the page. In the middle of the diamond he had written the word *Purpose*. At the points of the diamond were written four words. On the left was the word *Positive*, at the right was the word *Powerful*, on the top was the word *Simple* and the word *Serving* was at the bottom.

"Bob, an organization's purpose should be PPSS.

- Positive — an organization exists to contribute something positive to the world.

- Powerful — the purpose should inspire people to want to be part of it.

- Simple — it should be so simple that it is easily remembered.

- Serving — it should focus on serving a customer."

"Burns, I hate to the play the devil's advocate."

"Well, don't then. I've found he really doesn't need any help."

Bob grinned. "I'm going to anyway. This seems too simple. Surely your success isn't all due to one altruistic sounding sentence."

"No, it isn't. But that's the foundation. We've been pretty innovative but it's not like we're hurting for competition. Others can copy *what* we do and even *how* we do it. Our purpose is *why* we do what we do. And our competition hasn't successfully copied the *why*. The *why* is a lot more important than the *how* and the *what*."

"At the risk of making a bad pun, *why* is that?"

"It has everything to do with motivation. I'll give you an example, Bob. When I went off to college many moons ago I wore my boots, jeans and cowboy hat on campus. I'll never forget the first day I went to history class and the professor made fun of the way I was dressed. He accused me of being a *romantic*. You know what a romantic is?"

"Someone who is not grounded in reality — like Don Quixote."

"That was the professor's implication. But I looked romantic up in the dictionary and found this definition: 'Marked by the emotional appeal of the heroic, adventurous, remote, mysterious or idealized.'

"Have you ever thought about the power the image of the cowboy holds in our imaginations? It doesn't make any difference where you go in the world, the cowboy is revered. I remember being in Indonesia years ago with a group of beef producers on a trade mission. I walked into a restaurant wearing my hat and boots and the maitre d' ran up to me all excited and yelled, 'Clint Eastwood!'"

"Clint Eastwood?" Bob laughed. "That was awhile back wasn't it?"

"I was a lot younger then and Clint Eastwood was still alive. But the point is this — here it is 2030 but the cowboy aura is as powerful today as it was 150 years ago. It's still a popular subject of literature and film. Why do you suppose that is?"

"Maybe we're all romantics at heart."

"Go to the head of the class, Bob. The cowboy epitomizes romanticism. People are desperate to be part of something heroic and adventurous. The successful organization of the 20th century was defined by efficiency, economy of scale, consolidation, growth and innovation. But they reduced the role of people to little more than that of machines. Oh, they *talked* about people being the organization's most valuable asset but most of what they *did* said otherwise.

"There was nothing heroic, adventurous or idealized about their so-called 'missions.' For all intents and purposes there was no purpose — other than 'enhancing the shareholders' equity.'"

"Oh, come on now," Bob chided. "*They were kissing the customers lips until they were chapped.*"

Burns laughed. "Kind of liked that didn't you?"

"Well, that's an image you can't quite get out of your mind. But seriously, listening to you a person would think that you're saying financial performance isn't important."

"Of course it is. But let's go back to the bank example. Like too many organizations they got it bassackwards. They were so myopic that all of their focus was on the next quarter's financial performance. When you're driven from quarter to quarter you start force-feeding customers things they don't want or need. I learned that lesson when I worked in the pharmaceutical business. It was all about 'hitting our numbers' this quarter. The focus wasn't on the customer and no one talked about what we were doing as being 'heroic or adventurous.' Working purely for the sake of 'hitting the numbers' is just work with no meaning — other than survival. And if it's just about survival we're no different than any other animal."

"So, what makes Diamond Enterprises different?"

"Bob, I failed in business when I was just trying to survive. If you're focused on survival, you'll fail. If you're focused on serving you'll succeed.

"It all comes back to PPSS. An organization exists to make a *positive* contribution to the world. Its purpose must be so *powerful* that it incites and excites people enough to want to join the cause — to be part of something heroic and adventurous. It's all about *serving* other people. The only reason an organization exists — or an individual for that matter — is *to serve*. And those that do it best will be the most successful."

"And it's that *simple*?"

"Yes, Bob, it's that *simple*."

Once upon a time, riding pasture was part of the sum-mertime routine for a cowboy. He would count the cattle, rope and doctor any sick animals and repair fence as needed. But times had changed. For one thing, agriculture wasn't the male dominated domain it once was, as evidenced by Burns's foreman, Sandy Burton. And technology had made the handling of livestock less labor intensive, less stressful and more efficient. Newborn calves were implanted with a *nanochip*, which served as a microscopic identification system that held health records and other critical data. A reading of the chip could be made long distance via satellite. Branding cattle was no longer necessary to identify them. They were tracked and monitored 24 hours a day with a Global Positioning System which made cattle rustling nearly impossible.

Conventional fencing was giving way to some new high-tech forms. One involved using the nanochip as a mini version of an electrical shock collar. A florescent colored cable lying on the ground that was visible night and day established the boundary. The nanochip could be programmed to deliver a mild shock when an animal ventured too close to the cable. The barbed wire fence that Burns and Bob encountered was one of the few left on the ranch. Most post-and-wire cross fences on the ranch were being replaced by the high-tech versions.

Genetics had made quantum leaps in the last two decades, reducing the once numerous breeds to a select few composite hybrids. Due to genetic advances most disease problems were a thing of the past. So, for Bob and Burns riding pasture this morning was no more than an excuse to go for a pleasure ride. No counting, no roping, no doctoring and no fixing fence. But, as Burns so aptly put it, riding pasture was a lot more relaxing than playing golf.

The sun was high in the sky now as they headed back to headquarters. About a hundred yards from the barn Bob could see Sandy leaning against the corral fence waiting for them. About that time a gust of wind picked up an empty feed sack and blew it directly between old Buck's legs. He shied sideways and nearly crawled on top of the bay Burns was riding. By some strange quirk of fate Buck stuck one of his hind legs directly into the inside of the sack and he tried to get rid of it the only way he knew how. It looked like the rodeo was on after all.

Bob was caught off guard by the sack attack. He was riding with the reins slack and now Buck had his way with him. The big gelding's head went down, his hind legs went up and some daylight appeared between the seat of Bob's britches and the seat of the saddle. He searched for the saddle horn with one hand and jerked back on the reins with the other. Bob managed to keep his seat and the spontaneous saddle bronc event didn't last long. After two or three good bucks, Buck sent the sack sailing in the wind.

Once they saw that Bob was out of harm's way Burns and Sandy broke out laughing. Bob managed a nervous smile.

"Say cowboy, you didn't tell us you were a bronc rider!" Burns yelled. "You know, I wouldn't be a bit surprised if Sandy didn't plant that feed sack out here hoping for a little action out of Buck."

Bob eased down out of the saddle and handed the reins to Sandy.

"Don't believe him, Bob. He's always trying to start something. I couldn't have planned that if I'd wanted to."

"I'm just glad I didn't bite the dust. I would have never been able to show my face around here again if the horse the grandkids ride would have unloaded me."

Burns's satellite phone beeped. "Excuse me for minute. Sandy, could you keep an eye on *Broncho Bob* here for a minute?"

"Come on in the barn, Bob. I'll get us something cold to drink."

Bob was starting to feel like one of the family around here. Burns had to feel pretty comfortable with Bob or he wouldn't have kidded him so much. He found a seat on a feed barrel and Sandy returned with a couple of bottles of water.

"Burns says you grew up near here."

"Yes, but that was a long time ago."

"Well, you still have some cowboy left in you. Buck's no spring chicken but he pitched pretty good and you kept your seat."

"Well, as they say in Arkansas, even a blind hog finds an acorn every now and then. How long have you been with Diamond, Sandy?"

"About ten years."

"I know this is going to sound silly, but do you know what the purpose of Diamond Enterprises is?"

"Of course," she said matter-of-factly. "Our purpose is to feed a hungry world."

"Bob!" Burns hollered from outside.

"Sounds like the boss is ready to hit the trail, Sandy. Thanks for the water."

Sandy passed Bob's "purpose" test. She might have been tutored before Bob showed up but that didn't seem to be Burns's style — he might be a bit fanatical but he seemed to be genuine. Bob was betting Sandy's response was real and unrehearsed.

Bob knew he was only about one layer deep in peeling the onion. It was over lunch that the next layer would be revealed.

"Burns, I understand that discovering your purpose was the catalyst that launched Diamond Enterprises, but there has to be more to the story."

"You still have that piece of paper I gave you?"

"Sure." Bob reached inside his shirt pocket and handed it to Burns.

Burns turned the paper over and drew another diamond.

"Kind of fond of diamonds aren't you, Burns?"

"There's more than one way to look at a diamond, Bob. I've discovered that it's a good model for organizational development. You ever play baseball?"

"Are you kidding? Mickey Mantle is the patron saint of Oklahoma. Playing baseball is almost mandatory if you grew up here."

"Then you know baseball is played on a diamond. To score in baseball you have to touch all the bases." Burns wrote *Purpose* on the right hand side of the diamond, where first base would be.

"I look at Purpose as first base in organizational development. I figured out my purpose and that became first base in building Diamond Enterprises. The next challenge I faced in building a successful organization was people.

"The last half of the 20th Century saw a shift in workplace attitudes. The generation of workers whose formative years were spent in the Great Depression and in World War II became the work force of the post-war era. Twenty-five percent unemployment was prevalent throughout the depression years of 1930-1940. Then, during the war years of 1941-1945, many of this generation served in the armed forces. These post war workers were conditioned in a culture that revered security and authority. The organizational culture of most organizations was not unlike the military in which many of these workers served. In fact, the management style of that time could be described as paramilitary or authoritarian. Workers viewed the authoritarian culture as a tradeoff for the security they never had in the pre-war years of the Great Depression.

"At the turn of the century, Baby Boomers, the generation that was born in the nineteen years that followed World War II, were reaching middle age. Raised in the most affluent and secure era in history, they had a much different outlook than the previous generation. Baby Boomers came of age in the late sixties and early seventies when the so-called establishment was questioned and even disdained. So the old 'my way or the highway' management style was proving to be less than effective with them. There were a bunch of Boomers but the following generations weren't nearly as plentiful. Generations X, Y and Z grew up in an even more affluent and secure time than the Boomers and they sure didn't respond to the authoritarian management style. Add those things all together and one of the biggest problems organizations faced was figuring out how to find, hire and keep good people.

"Some business gurus of the day were saying that full-time workers employed exclusively by one outfit might become a thing of the past. In other words, they were predicting a contract workforce — kind of a 'have skills, will travel' arrangement. It sounded pretty far-fetched at the time but the more I thought about it, the more it made sense to me. It just seemed to be a solution whose time had not yet come."

"So, you had to figure out how to bridge the gap, right?"

"Right. I struggled with that for a long time. Then I realized the answer was really one that's been in existence since the beginning of time." Burns wrote the word *Partner* above second base on the diamond. "I remember something that Peter Drucker said back then, 'The greatest change in corporate culture and the way business is being conducted may be the accelerated growth of relationships based on partnership.' I learned that when Peter Drucker spoke, you'd do well to listen. That made sense to me. Shoot, I'd partnered a lot with people on cattle deals.

"I used to feed cattle with a man out in southwestern Kansas. He was one of those people you liked to hang out with just to soak up his wisdom. He headed up the largest family-owned agribusiness enterprise in the state and he did it largely by forming strategic partnerships. His philosophy was that it was better to have a little bit of a lot as opposed to a lot of a little bit. That philosophy enabled him to multiply himself through a lot of other people. And the neat thing about it was that he helped the people he partnered with accomplish things that they never could have on their own. Instead of each of them fighting the other to get the biggest piece of the pie, they collectively made the pie bigger."

"That runs contrary to human nature, Burns," interjected Bob. "We tend to be pretty independent — not to mention greedy."

"I didn't say it was easy. But you'll never accomplish anything of greatness on your own. All of us have strengths — and weaknesses. An effective partnership allows people to capitalize on their strengths. Even the Lone Ranger didn't go it alone — he partnered with Tonto.

"I learned something else from another old cattleman. He told me there are three reasons you might need a partner — if you need money, or if you need labor, or if you need expertise.

Those are the three essential elements of a partnership. If you have one, or even two of the three, you're still going to be short a leg on a three legged stool. So, a partnership is a way to supply the missing element."

"But you can hire labor and expertise, Burns. And if you need money you can borrow it."

"That's true. But think of the advantages of partnering versus hiring or borrowing."

"Well, the obvious advantage is a sense of ownership. People pay attention when they have an investment at risk. But I've seen a lot more partnerships fail than succeed."

"And I can tell you why, Bob. No purpose. If it's *just* about making money then it's a wreck waiting to happen."

"So, how *did* you form your partnerships?"

"First of all, there was no way I was going to feed a hungry world by myself. Our ranch was just a small part of one segment of one industry within the food industry. So I had to find other operations in all segments of the beef industry that had come to the realization that they needed to be part of a *virtually integrated* partnership."

"OK, you lost me. I know what vertical integration is but what do you mean when you say *virtually* integrated?"

"The beef industry was too fragmented for one conglomerate to take the product from conception to the dinner plate. There were too many individuals and companies spread over too much geography to make that work. Besides, it would take trillions of dollars to finance it even if it could be done. The trend was to become part of an alliance that would virtually integrate. Think of it as being a *collaboration* instead of a *conglomeration*. Diamond Enterprises began as an alliance of partners who wanted to be part of something collectively bigger than the sum of the individual parts."

"That's the definition of synergism, Burns."

"That's right."

"But you said the trend was to form alliances," Bob continued. "If there were other alliances how did you convince them to be part of yours?"

"They had to buy into the purpose of feeding a hungry world. If they didn't, that was the deal breaker. I wanted hunger fighters — people whose focus was on serving instead of survival. And they had to buy into that regardless of what segment they represented in the food chain. All of us ultimately had to satisfy the end-product consumer."

"So you recruited beef producers. But Diamond produces all types of food products. How did that happen?"

"It was the next logical step. The food industry is the largest industry in the world. It provides the most fundamental of all human needs as well as one of our greatest sources of pleasure. Agriculture is the ground floor of the food industry. But just like with the beef producers, most of agriculture was too fragmented. Producers were mostly independent entrepreneurs. If they weren't family owned most had evolved from family ownership. Their independence — and a misguided sense of pride in that independence — was what held them back. We had to help them understand they weren't just in the beef business or the grain business but that they were an integral part of the food business."

"I'll bet you had people beating down your door to sign on."

"You'd be surprised, Bob. Some people just didn't get it. They were so wrapped up in their own little worlds and how they had always done things in the past that they couldn't grasp the concept of *interdependence*."

"So, what did they do?"

"They went broke."

"And Diamond kept getting bigger. But I want to get back to what you said about not having full-time employees. Surely you have people who fit in that category don't you?"

"Yes, but not in the *traditional* sense."

VII

Traditional. On one hand Burns Marcus was the most traditional of men — a self-described "old cowboy" who preferred riding pasture over playing golf. On the other hand he was the most unconventional businessman Bob had ever met. He embraced new technology with a passion that would have made Bill Gates jealous — at least back when Bill Gates was young and in his prime. Burns Marcus was a unique combination of old and new school — an old timer who was way ahead of his time. Bob wanted to know how Burns solved the full-time employee riddle. It was time to peel another layer of the onion.

"How did you bridge the gap?"

"You mean the gap between having full-time versus contract employees?"

"Yes. I see how you built a virtual organization but there have to be functions that require full-time employees."

"Bob, what do people want from their work?"

Bob had to think for a minute. "Money, security, benefits, retirement... I guess those are the main things."

"Do you know people whose jobs provide those things?"

"Sure I do," Bob looked a little perplexed. "Burns, every company offers those things to employees nowadays."

"Does it make them happy?"

"More or less."

"Well, which is it? *More* or *less*?"

"I don't think most people necessarily associate *happiness* with *work*."

"Why not?"

"Hey, wait a minute. Who's conducting the interview here anyway?"

Burns laughed. "OK, I'll back off for now. But I'm not letting you off the hook. I'll come back to the happiness question later.

"I decided the issue wasn't full-time *versus* contract employees. When I worked for the pharmaceutical company we used to have monthly sales meetings. I used to share a ride with a younger salesman to and from the meetings. We'd drive in the night before and drive home the night after the meeting. I remember one night on our way home from the meeting he asked me how I felt about the company making us travel to and from the meetings on 'our own time.' I told him I didn't see it that way. I never looked at it as 'company time' and 'my time.' It was all 'my time.' I viewed it as me simply *contracting* my services with the company as a salesman. I never looked at hours, I looked at results. If it took eight hours or twenty hours a day to get the job done that was *my choice*. If I didn't like the hours or the results I could always contract my services with another outfit."

"Or go out on your own."

"And that's exactly what I ended up doing. Either way it was my choice. And everybody has a choice. Nobody's forcing anybody to work anywhere. If you think about it, *everyone* who works for an organization is a contract employee. The real issue revolves around how the contract is structured. So I decided to apply the partnering principle to employees."

Bob looked perplexed. "So, you make *employees* partners?"

"Remember the three essential elements of a partnership, Bob?"

"You said they were labor, expertise and money."

"That's right. Most employees come to work seeking money. In exchange they offer labor and expertise. Companies typically dictate all the terms of the contract. We'll supply X number of dollars and you'll work Y number of hours.

"We decided to treat prospective employees as potential partners. Every individual brings something unique to the partnership. They each want different things out of the partnership. So we structure the partnership on the basis of that uniqueness."

"OK Burns, but what if they want to work different hours or want more money than you offer? What if an employee wants to take off to watch their kids play ball? Who covers for them?"

"Whoa, Bob… one question at a time. I used to feed cattle with a guy up in Nebraska who had a unique approach to deal with all of the problems you just brought up. He found he had some people who wanted to work more hours and some less. So he let the employees work out their schedules with each other."

"But what about conflict… I mean what if somebody wasn't happy with the deal."

"My friend in Nebraska found that a jury of your peers is more fair and equitable than a judge. They worked it out. I borrowed a page from his playbook and we created teams that performed different functions. Then we let the teams work out their schedules. Everybody is at a different place in life. Some are single, some married, some have kids. Are their kids toddlers, school age or have they flown the coop? People have to make tradeoffs in time and money depending on where they are in their lives. They can make more money not just by how much time they invest but also by how much risk they're willing to take. We can structure the partnership with more or less risk. We structure the partnership to be dynamic — it's reviewed on a regular basis."

"So, it sounds like you treat each new hire, or partnership as an individual deal."

"It *is* an individual deal — *especially for that individual.*"

"So, what's the main thing you look for in forming an employee partnership?"

"Several things. Do they share our values — integrity, professionalism, caring, stewardship and quality? And there's one other thing…"

"Let me guess… they have to buy into the purpose."

"You're a quick study, Bob. We spend a lot of time talking with them about being part of something that's heroic, adventurous and idealistic."

"Your history professor was right, Burns. You *are* a romantic."

"I plead guilty but I'm unrepentant. If our purpose of 'feeding a hungry world' doesn't get their blood pumping then we know their motivation will be limited to the things you said people typically want from their work."

"You mean money, security, benefits, retirement…"

"Right. Now let's get back to my question of 'do you think that makes them happy?' You said people don't necessarily associate happiness with work. Is that right?"

"Well, that's what I said. I think it's sad but true."

Burns walked over to the fireplace and picked up an old branding iron that was leaning against the hearth. "Bob, in the old west a ranch branded their livestock as a way to identify them. But that brand had far more significance to the people who worked for the ranch. The brand was sort of like a coat of arms or a family crest.

"If you worked for the Rocking R outfit, for example, you rode for the Rocking R brand. You *were* the Rocking R, as far as other people were concerned. That was a source of pride among the cowboys who worked there. They spoke well of the Rocking R, stood up for the Rocking R and, if need be, they fought for the Rocking R."

"And you're looking for people who want to ride for the brand."

"We're looking for people," Burns said as he eyed the diamond shaped end of the branding iron, "who want to ride for the *Diamond* brand — because they believe that what we're doing is heroic, adventurous and idealistic."

Riding for the brand. Was Burns Marcus a hopeless romantic — a modern day Don Quixote in a pair of cowboy boots? The facts said otherwise. Bob knew leaders of successful enterprises were sometimes so close to the leading edge that they were occasionally accused of being over the edge. Wal-Mart founder Sam Walton was known for leading Wal-Mart associates in the Wal-Mart cheer and once did a dance in a hula skirt on Wall Street. Southwest Airlines CEO, Herb Kelleher, once engaged in a good natured arm-wrestling match with a competitor to settle a trademark dispute. Bob could see some of the traits of these corporate giants of yesteryear in Burns Marcus. He was not only an innovator — he had plowed new ground in the field of human motivation.

"Burns, I don't know how to say this, but to hard-nosed business people your 'riding for the brand' philosophy sounds a little, uh..."

"Hokey? Touchy-feely?"

"Well... "

"It's OK. I understand. Thirty years ago I would have said the same thing. Good business people trust in things they can count, measure and weigh. And believe me we count, measure and weigh everything, too. That's just sound business. If you don't, you can't stay in business. So that's the ante in the poker game of production. If you want to play you have to ante up. But once you get past that, what differentiates the good from the better and the better from the best? It's how you handle the people side of business.

"You know what drives bean counters nuts? Things that are *difficult* to count, measure and weigh. And it's hard to measure human motivation and how it affects the bottom line. Human motivation is intangible. You can't stick a thermometer in someone's mouth and say, 'Well, it looks like you're 100% motivated!' So, what do we tend to do about things that are intangible?"

"We discount them."

"That's right. We spend all of our time and energy on things that *can be* counted, measured and weighed — the tangibles. That's what shows up in the annual report."

"But don't the intangibles have an effect on the tangibles?"

"Bob, you've hit on the thing that separates leaders from managers. Managers understand the tangibles. Leaders understand the *intangibles*.

"I have to be a good manager just to *survive* in business. But I have to be a good leader to *thrive* in business.

"If you want people to ride for the brand you have to build a purpose-driven organization. And that takes purposeful leadership."

"So, how do you *define* purposeful leadership?"

51

"Well, I hate to have to admit it but it's something I read in the professional provoker's book. It revolves around his fundamental tenet of human behavior: 'Without a purpose our only motivation is reward and punishment.' I found that to be an effective leader you have to understand what motivates *you*. If you can understand what motivates *you* then you can understand what motivates *others*."

"But isn't that different for everybody? I mean aren't people motivated by different things?"

"Yes… and no."

"What do you mean?"

"Well, we all are motivated by many different things but you can put them all into three basic categories."

"Let me guess… reward, punishment and, of course, I know you'd say purpose. But I have to disagree."

"OK, what would *you* say?"

"That all motivation would fall into just two categories — reward and punishment."

"Before I read the provoker's book I would have agreed with you. But he pointed out something that anybody who grew up around livestock would know."

"What's that?"

"Let's go back down to the barn and I'll show you."

The sun was getting low in the sky now. It reminded Bob of something his grandpa used to tell him. That once the sun reached a certain point just above the horizon it would hit a slick spot. When it hit that slick spot the sun went down fast. By the time they reached the barn the sun was just about to hit the slick spot.

Burns walked into the barn, grabbed a bucket and scooped it half-full of oats from the feed barrel Bob had perched on earlier that day when he had visited with Sandy.

"Come on, Bob. Let's see if we can entice old Buck back up to the barn."

Sandy had turned the horses out into a small pasture on the west side of the barn. As Bob looked to the far side of the pasture he could see the silhouette of old Buck and the bay framed by the rapidly setting sun. Burns held the bucket up above his head, rattled it a bit and whistled. The two horses, which had been grazing peacefully, jerked up their heads simultaneously and pointed their ears directly at Burns. He rattled the bucket again and whistled. That's all it took. The horses closed the distance between them and the men just as the sun hit the slick spot. Burns dumped the oats in a feed bunk and the horses gobbled up their evening snack.

Bob couldn't help himself. Even though old Buck had tried to unload him earlier that day, he had to reach out and let his hand run across the buckskin's glossy coat. It was a feel that brought back fond memories of his days growing up horseback.

"You know Bob, watching you reminds me of something Ronald Reagan said."

"What's that?"

"There is nothing so good for the inside of a man as the outside of a horse."

Bob smiled as he stroked Buck's slick hide, "I can't argue with that."

After a late supper, Bob, Jane and Burns found themselves back on the porch, each occupying a rocking chair. The conversation was sparse. Burns was just about talked out and Bob was content to reflect on his day in silence. The locusts seemed to join in with the creaking of the rockers to perform an evening serenade.

Bob was here to write a story but he was beginning to feel like he was part of the story he was writing. Today when he was riding pasture with Burns it was if he was caught in that time warp again. And now, while he was sitting on the porch, seduced by the sounds of the night, it occurred to him that he had completely forgotten about the object lesson Burns was going to give him on purposeful leadership. His sense of duty kicked back in. He had to stay on task.

"Burns, when we headed for the barn you were going to tell me more about purposeful leadership. You must have gotten sidetracked while feeding the horses."

"I didn't get sidetracked. I gave you the lesson."

Bob stopped his rocking. "Then I must be dumber than a box of rocks. I don't get it."

"It'll keep, Bob. What do you say we talk about it tomorrow?"

Bob was in no mood to argue. Burns and old Buck had just about worn him out. As grandpa would say, he felt like he had been rode hard and put up wet. He closed his eyes and listened to the locusts joined by the creaking rhythm of his rocker.

VIII

Bob hobbled into the kitchen and found Burns facing the window taking in the morning ritual of the quail parading across the lawn.

"Say, cowboy, you're walking a little bowlegged this morning."

"I told you I'd be saddle sore," Bob said as he poured himself a cup of coffee. "And that was before I knew you'd entered me in the saddle bronc ridin'."

"You did yourself proud, Bob. You even impressed Sandy — and she's not easily impressed. But I think she was pretty impressed with you *before* you ever got on old Buck."

Bob smiled. He was pretty impressed with Sandy, too, but he didn't feel like putting on any riding clinic today. "Well, if it's all the same to you, I'd just as soon skip riding pasture this morning."

Burns shrugged. "If you insist. What would you like to do?"

"I want to pick back up where we left off last night. When I asked you about purposeful leadership, you said you'd 'show me' and hauled me off to the barn. But all we did was feed the horses."

"Bob, when you were growing up did you ever try to catch a horse out in the pasture?"

"Sure."

"How'd you go at it?"

"Same as you did last night."

"Ever try it without the feed bucket? Did you ever just grab a bridle or a halter and walk out into the pasture and try to catch a horse?"

"Yes... and the chase was on. The horse knew that if a bridle was in my hand a saddle couldn't be far behind."

"OK, that's part one of your object lesson on purposeful leadership."

"That if I want to catch the horse I've got to take the feed bucket?"

"Yes. Now you're ready for part two."

"I'm not sure I understand part one."

Burns laughed, "You will. Just hang with me." Burns walked over to the kitchen counter, opened a drawer and pulled out what Bob recognized as a dog training collar and tossed it onto the table. "Know what that is?"

"It's a shock collar."

"That's right. You know how it works?"

"You put it on a dog and use a battery operated remote control. When the dog does something you don't want it to do, you push a button on the remote and it shocks the dog."

"And after you repeat the process a few times, Bob, the dog learns not to do that anymore. That's part two of the lesson on purposeful leadership."

"Burns, I don't see what any of this has got to do with purposeful leadership."

"Sure you do. Anybody who has spent any time working with animals understands that you train them using reward and punishment."

"OK, I get the point. We feed the horse and it'll come running. We shock the dog and send it running. So you're saying the best way to motivate people is to use the carrot instead of the stick. And *that's* purposeful leadership, right?"

"No. That's *not* purposeful leadership. Think about it, Bob. You can train a horse, a cow, a hog or a dog using reward and punishment. It's a matter of stimulus and response. If I try to motivate *people* with reward and punishment I'm not a leader, I'm just an animal trainer."

"But what's wrong with rewarding people? Isn't that a *positive* way to motivate them?"

"Yes, but reward has its limitations. Let's say that I pay you a specific amount of money to perform a specific task. Now I ask you to perform the task faster or more efficiently or maybe to take on more tasks. What do you expect in return?"

"I'll expect more money."

"If money is your primary motivation what's eventually going to happen?"

"You're either going to run out of money or I'm going to run out of motivation. But there are other ways of rewarding people than just money — like recognition, pats on the back, things that are intangible."

"And there's nothing wrong with that either. We all can use a pat on the back and everyone appreciates recognition if it's deserved and genuine — but it's still extrinsic motivation. It's an external stimulus. When I read the professional provoker's book he explained that, like other animals, humans have needs. He used Maslow's hierarchy as an example. You probably remember Maslow's hierarchy from Psychology 101 in college."

"Sure. Maslow said that we have different levels of needs. If I remember right, the basic needs are food, shelter and security."

"That's right. Maslow said that once those needs are filled we graduate to psychological needs like love and acceptance. Then we move on to the 'pat on the back' as you so aptly put it — the need for recognition, competence and achievement. When I worked for the pharmaceutical company I collected a wall full of plaques for sales achievement — you know, because I 'hit the numbers.' I have no idea where those plaques are today. After awhile hanging another plaque on the wall was meaningless. And after I'd won so many sales trips, it became a matter of 'been there, done that.' Those things just didn't trip my trigger anymore."

"You obviously found a better way to motivate people. How'd you do it?"

"I backed into it. I first had to figure out what motivated me. I'd done the reward and punishment thing in my corporate tour of duty. That's how most organizations try to motivate people — the carrot and the stick. All the research I studied on the subject revealed that the overwhelming majority of people in the workplace were *unmotivated*. And you know what the definition of insanity is, don't you?"

Bob nodded, "Doing the same thing over and over but expecting different results."

"Right — and that's what I saw organizations doing. So if reward and punishment weren't the answer, what was? For me the answer was the discovery of my purpose. But that was *my* purpose — as an individual. Then I related that back to my work experience with the pharmaceutical company. What was missing? No sense of purpose."

"But your company had a mission statement didn't it?"

"Come on, Bob. You told me that nobody pays any attention to mission statements, remember?"

"Uh, yeah… because they were like your bank's mission statement… a lot of verbiage without a lot of meaning."

"Uh-huh. Most organizations are not as mission-driven as they'd like to think they are. They're typically personality-driven, crisis-driven or combinations of both. A crisis-driven organization is motivated from crisis to crisis. During a crisis everyone is motivated to solve the crisis. But once the crisis subsides so does the motivation — until there's another crisis."

"How about the personality-driven organization?"

"Many very successful organizations are founded by dynamic, charismatic people. They embody the 'purpose' in their personality. While the purpose of the organization may not be exactly clear, it is personified in their very being. They are evangelists who preach the gospel of their cause to employees, investors and customers. The problem is that the founder isn't going to be around forever. So when he or she kicks the bucket the 'purpose' gets buried with them. It may take years for it to die completely but it invariably does.

"I decided that I was going to build a purpose-driven organization. We all want to give ourselves to something that's bigger than ourselves as individuals. Diamond Enterprises isn't about me — it's about the purpose of feeding a hungry world. Diamond Enterprises' purpose was simply an extension of my personal purpose. My number one job is to be the head hunger fighter and to preach that gospel daily. If I can't get our partners to buy into that purpose, then I've failed. And if that purpose doesn't outlive me, then I've failed."

"I understand people wanting to give themselves to something bigger than themselves, Burns. But what about *me* as an individual? If I'm here just to serve Diamond's purpose then it seems like I'm just a mind-numbed robot here to do your bidding."

"Bob, you're ready for part three of purposeful leadership. Do you remember the highest need on Maslow's hierarchy?"

"It had something to do with human potential, didn't it?"

"That's pretty close. He called it Self-Actualization — the need to fulfill our own unique potential. It's not enough for people to buy into the corporate purpose. If everything we do is just for the company and we're just cogs in the wheel, then we're no different than a cult. A hundred years ago that's how Adolf Hitler sold his Nazi bill of goods to the German people. As individuals they were nothing. They were to sacrifice themselves for the 'fatherland.' And of course, he established himself as the supreme being of the fatherland. They were committed to something bigger than themselves and they followed it blindly. But it shows how desperately the human species seeks meaning for their existence — even to the point of giving themselves over to something evil."

Bob leaned forward. "What's all that got to do with self-actualization?"

"Well, it has to do with the leadership of the organization. I'm not saying there are a bunch of Hitlers running companies but I am saying there are a lot of companies that suffer from narcissistic management. Narcissistic managers think the world revolves around them and what *they* want. Those managers often expect everyone else to sacrifice themselves for the good of the company — the company being synonymous with them. But it doesn't have to be that way. People want to give themselves to something bigger than they are but they also want to fulfill their own unique potential. Purposeful leaders are able to help people connect the dots between the individual's purpose and the organization's purpose."

"So," Bob said, "the way the organization reaches its full potential is by helping its people reach *their* full potential. But most people don't even think in the terms that you use, Burns. If you told people that they can find self-actualization in their work they'd look at you like you said you were going to send them to the moon."

"You realize, of course, that going to the moon isn't a big deal anymore, Bob. People do it all the time."

"Oh, you know what I mean. That was just a figure of speech."

"But you inadvertently made a good point, Bob. Space travel is now a commonly accepted mode of transportation. Humankind has mastered so many frontiers of technology and yet we still struggle with the people part of business. And every business is in the people business. Remember what you said when I asked you what makes people happy at work?"

"I said they didn't necessarily associate happiness with work."

"They do when they are self-actualizing."

"You mean reaching their full potential?"

"Yep, and can you imagine what happens to productivity when you have an organization of self-actualizing people?"

"Oh," Bob said with a hint of sarcasm, "I suspect you'd harness enough energy to send them to the moon."

"I like your sense of humor, Bob. But in all seriousness, that's what you get when you have a self-actualizing organization — unbelievable energy. In fact, I've even come up with a term for it. I call it *Team-Actualization*."

"Team-Actualization? What does *that* mean?"

"Well Bob, I think I can give you an example you'll relate to. You've already proven yourself to be a pretty fair bronc rider. Ever do much ropin'?"

"To be honest, I used to be a pretty fair roper."

"Really?" Burns raised his eyebrows. "Care to prove it?"

"Oh no, you're not going to put me back in the saddle again."

"Come on and be a sport, Bob. Sandy's got a few steers down at the arena for us to chase. You wouldn't mind seeing Sandy again would you?"

"Holding out the carrot, eh Burns?"

Burns picked up the shock collar and jokingly asked, "Would you rather I use this?"

Bob stood up and walked to the door. He swung it open with one hand and made a sweeping gesture with the other. "After you, Burns, I'd love to see Sandy again."

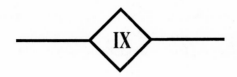

IX

Like most rodeo events, team roping's origins can be traced back to actual work performed on ranches. It was the way cowboys worked cattle on the open range. With no pens or chutes available, they relied on one of the most useful tools in the cowboy's arsenal — the lariat. One cowboy would rope the animal's head and another cowboy would rope the hind legs. Stretched out on the ground between the two horses the animal was effectively restrained so the cowboys could brand or doctor. The practice became commonly referred to as *headin' and heelin'*. In competitive team roping, whoever ropes the head is referred to as the "header" and the "heeler" takes care of the other end.

Sandy was waiting at the arena when Burns pulled up in a cloud of dust. Bob eyed her suspiciously as he crawled out of the pickup.

"Are there any strategically placed feed sacks in the arena?" he asked.

"Now, Bob, you're not suggesting that I instigated your last foray into the world of rodeo are you?" she asked with a somewhat devious smile. "You act like a gun-shy bird dog."

Bob had just finished his shock collar lesson. Now Sandy compares him to a gun-shy bird dog. He wondered if he should start barking.

"No, Sandy, I'm just a sack-shy writer. You're not packing a gun are you? Or firecrackers or anything else that might cause a horse to break in two?"

"Nope. I'm going to offer up a disclaimer. Anything that happens in this arena is either of your own doing or an act of God. You got a problem with that and you can take it up with him."

"Fair enough."

While Bob and Sandy bantered back and forth, Burns just leaned against the pickup and smiled. He was starting to realize that he could have climbed back into the pickup and driven off and they probably wouldn't have even noticed. "I hate to interrupt you two but what do you say we rope a few steers?"

"Let's do it." Bob was not only relaxed, but was anxious to rope. It was if he had reverted to a former life and assumed another identity.

"Did you ever rope competitively, Bob?"

"Burns," Bob drawled with a bit of an attitude, "I went to college on a rodeo scholarship. *My event was team ropin'.*"

"Well, I'll be... which end?"

"I could rope both ends but heelin' was my thing."

"What a coincidence. Old Buck is a made-to-order heelin' horse and I'm a pretty fair header. Think you and old Buck can hold up your end of the deal?"

"There's only one way to find out."

Sandy already had the horses saddled and the steers in the chute. Bob and Burns mounted up, loped around the arena a couple of times and backed into their respective boxes on either side of the chute. Sandy tripped the gate which released the steer and the chase was on. The bay gelding was out quick and put Burns in perfect position. Burns made a clean catch of the steer's horns and turned off sharp to the left. Old Buck proved himself to be a good heelin' horse indeed and placed Bob right on the steer's tail. Bob swung his rope, getting in rhythm with the steer's hind legs as they bounded up and down off the arena dirt. One, two, three… he threw… and caught nothing but air. Bob's face turned red. He quickly built another loop for a second throw. This time he *double-hocked* him. Bob let the rope go slack, the steer got up, kicked out of the heel loop and Burns trailed it to the catch pen at the end of the arena. After fishing his loop off the steer's horns he rode back up along side of Bob and slapped him on the back. "Well, you *are* a heeler, Bob!"

"Took two loops," Bob offered half-apologetically.

"Why, how long has it been since you roped, son?"

"I don't know, a *long* time."

"Then I wouldn't complain. Kind of like ridin' a bike isn't it? You're just a little rusty. Let's rope a few more."

After roping a few more steers, Bob started getting back in form. Then Burns turned to Bob and asked, "What do you think, cowboy — ready to call it quits?"

"I think so. It's been fun but now I've got a sore arm to match my sore butt from my bronc ride."

"OK, but before we do I want you to try something."

"What's that?"

"I want you to rope a steer by yourself."

"But I've never done any steer trippin'."

"That's not what I meant."

"You mean just head a steer and turn it loose?"

"No. I'm gonna have Sandy turn a steer out and I want you to heel it."

"Without you headin' it first?"

"That's right."

"Burns, that's nuts." Bob swept off his hat and wiped the sweat from his forehead with his forearm. "Are you pulling my leg? It would be just dumb luck if I heeled a steer in an open arena unless someone ropes the head first."

"No," Burns laughed. "I'm trying to make a point. Just give it a go."

Here he goes again, Bob thought. *This is another object lesson.* "If you really want me to," Bob said as he rode Buck into the box.

Bob gave Sandy a nod and she tripped the gate. After a lap around the arena and a couple of unsuccessful throws, Bob coiled up his rope and trotted back to the chute. "OK, what's the point?"

"Let's go get some supper and we'll talk about it."

Once again, Burns left Bob hanging over the edge of the cliff. He seemed to enjoy making Bob jump through philosophical hoops to make his points. Bob couldn't protest too much — after all it would make for one interesting story. Once it was written, Bob knew he would have something that would make readers sit up and pay attention.

Meanwhile, back at the ranch, Jane had supper waiting for them. Bob was starting to feel like he was at home.

"OK, Burns. We were talking about *Team-Actualization* when you dragged me off to go *team roping.* Now, what's roping got to do with it?"

"Jane, you would have been real proud of Bob, here. Hadn't thrown a rope since old Shep was a pup and I'll be danged if he didn't look like a pro."

Jane gave Bob a knowing look. "He wears you out, doesn't he? Believe me I know. I put up with him every day. I never get a straight answer out of him. He always answers a question with a question or says, 'Let me show you something.' I swear Burns. Cut the man some slack. He's here to write a story, not be a ranch hand."

"Oh, I don't mind so long as we get to where we need to go," Bob said as he pushed back from the table. "Besides, I'm beginning to think I might want to hire on here. The food's good and you've got the best-looking ranch foreman I've ever seen."

"See there, Jane? Bob's not complaining. And I'll tell you something else, Bob. Sandy can put both of us to shame headin' *or* heelin'. Now, where was I?"

"Team-Actualization," Bob and Jane answered in unison. They all laughed.

"Yes, well... first of all, Bob, I'll bet you can see the obvious correlation between team roping and Team-Actualization."

"Well, you have two people working together for a common purpose. Something they couldn't accomplish individually. It's a pretty good metaphor for your partnership principle, too."

"Well put. Now, for *the rest of the story* as Paul Harvey used to say. Back when I was getting Diamond up and running I picked up a paper and read a story about motivation in the workplace. The article cited a study that found over half of employees in the workforce exhibited no enthusiasm for their work and that about one-fifth were so negative that their employers would have been better off to pay them to stay home. Imagine the impact this had on the bottom line. But how do you suppose those organizations typically tried to motivate these employees?"

"Well, they probably wouldn't have admitted it, but in simple terms it would be reward and punishment."

"That's right. Why weren't the people who were running these companies saying, 'Hey, we're spending billions to motivate our people and it isn't working. What's missing?' It seemed to me that if that wasn't working they ought to admit it and try something else. It was somewhere around the same time that I read another article in a magazine that posed these questions, 'When employees say they want to bring their whole selves to work, what does that mean? And what should employers do about it?' That's when I started thinking about applying what I knew about training animals to motivating people. It became painfully evident to me what these organizations were missing."

"And what was that?"

"In simple terms, as you appropriately put it, they were appealing to people's needs and/or fears using reward and/or punishment. Reward and punishment work great if you're training animals and since humans are animals we will respond to these stimuli but with minimal success."

"Like the feed bucket or the shock collar," Bob said.

"Exactly. But there is something unique about the human species that separates us from other animals. Our animal bodies house the *human spirit*. While our animal bodies will respond to the manipulation of reward and punishment, the human spirit responds to no external stimuli. We are the only animals that can be *intrinsically* motivated. We are created to fulfill a specific purpose in life. When intrinsic motivation is missing in our work then reward and punishment are our only motives. We naturally want to give ourselves to a cause — something bigger than ourselves. *Team-Actualization* is what happens when we contribute our singularly unique purposes to a *common* purpose — a greater cause.

"Employees bring their 'whole selves' to work every day. If people find no purpose in their work, then only their bodies are engaged — not their spirits. That's why people exhibited no enthusiasm for their work. Organizations were trying to motivate humans the same way you would train any animal while completely ignoring the one *motive* that is unique to our species — purpose. Enthusiasm comes from the Greek word for inspired — entheos. En (within) + Theos (God) means God within. If you want enthusiastic people you have to appeal to the part of them that is God — their spirit. Then the 'whole person' comes to work everyday."

"Burns, you sound like a preacher."

Burns laughed. "You're not the first person to accuse me of that. But trust me, Bob, I'm no preacher. I'm a businessman. I've got a bottom line to think about. We have to 'hit the numbers' like everybody else."

"But," Bob objected, "you're going to be accused of bringing religion in the workplace. It's *politically incorrect*."

"Bob, I gave up on being politically correct years ago. Besides, I read something Spencer Johnson said that supported my approach."

"Spencer Johnson?"

"Years ago he wrote a great book called *Who Moved My Cheese?* It was about a couple of mice that… well, it would take too long to explain. Anyway, I read where Spencer Johnson said 'research may one day show that the only long-lasting motivation will come from employees who bring it to work with them in the form of God, spirituality, or something else that causes them to rise to a *higher purpose*.' I believe the on-the-job research we've done here at Diamond Enterprises proves that he was right on target. We know people bring their whole selves to work every day and we've created a culture that appeals to a 'higher purpose' — a culture that engages their spirits as well as their bodies. That's the *power* of purposeful leadership.

"Think of it like this. All of an organization's resources must be maximized if it is to succeed. A resource represents potential. So let's think of an organization's human resources as 'human potential.' Imagine human potential as an iceberg. We all learned in grade school that what we see on the surface represents only a fraction of an iceberg. Most of the iceberg lies beneath the surface. Now, let's apply that to human potential. When we look at people all we see is the tip of the iceberg — their animal bodies — not the 'whole person.' The real potential lies beneath the surface — the human spirit. In order to maximize the human potential, we must appeal not only to the surface, that which we see, but to the part which we do not see, the spirit."

"But not everybody is going to buy into your spiritual-based theory of motivation, Burns."

"That's, OK. Organizations that fail to acknowledge the spiritual component will never come close to maximizing the potential of their human resources. They use reward and punishment like drugs. I guess you could call it institutional addiction. One of the steps in any 12-step rehabilitation program is to admit you need help from a higher power. It only made sense to me to approach human motivation from a psychological, scientific, and yes, a spiritual perspective. Humans intuitively seek meaning for their existence. All other animals are just trying to eat and keep from being eaten. We are the only animals that possess the power to *choose* our behavior."

"But what's *that* got to do with roping?"

"Our animal bodies die and decompose. Ancient Egyptians tried to preserve the body through the process of mummification. They thought so little of the brain that they removed it prior to this process. They believed that the *heart* was the seat of the intellect, the will and the emotions. Science has proven that the brain is the neurological control center. The head houses the brain but it is the human spirit — our heart — that exercises our free will.

"Consider this fundamental principle of livestock handling. Control the head and you control the animal. When we are motivated intrinsically it comes from the heart. Our intellect, will and emotions are channeled into actions via the brain. Other animals have brains but that's not where the power of choice is exercised. You will never beat your animal body into submission. It must be led. That's how we rise above our animal natures and become motivated from the inside out instead of outside in.

"When I asked you to heel a steer by yourself, you thought it was an exercise in futility. Right?"

"I *proved* it was an exercise in futility. It was all backwards. Why not do it the right way? Catch the head then you control the steer."

"And you're right. Even if you caught both heels, it's inefficient. You'd be working on the wrong end of the steer. That's what so many organizations are doing, Bob. They're working on the wrong end of human potential — the animal body. The key to having engaged, enthusiastic people is to appeal to the part of them that houses their enthusiasm — their hearts. Anyway you cut it, only human beings have the gift of free will — the power of choice. Call it spirituality or whatever you like. It's a matter of the heart. *Appeal to the heart and the head will follow.*"

"And when you control the head," Bob added, "you control the animal."

"It's amazing what you can learn from roping isn't it, Bob?"

B ob was engaged in what had become his morning ritual at the kitchen window — watching the quail parade across the lawn in the dawn's early light. He sipped slowly on his coffee and lingered at the kitchen window longer than he planned. He would miss this — drinking coffee and watching the quail. Once again he felt caught in that time warp — *and he liked it*. He didn't want to leave.

His body was aching from the rugged routine Burns had put him through but it was the kind of hurt that felt good. He had burned the midnight oil working on articles many times but his mind still raced after he went to bed. His time at the Marcus ranch had reminded him of when he was young, when after a long day of hard work he fell asleep nearly as soon as his head hit the pillow.

Here he was, once again longing for the past. While Bob was fighting his urge to roll back the clock, Burns Marcus seemed to be winding his watch forward. He had not only adapted to the ever-changing world of the 21st century — he reveled in being its pacesetter. How'd he do it? He'd ask him. But he had to find him first. Did he leave the house without him this morning? All was quiet except for a rhythmic creaking coming from somewhere outside. It had to be the rocker.

He found Burns in his rocker on the porch with his nose buried in a book. Maybe he was contemplating retirement and would prove to be human after all.

"So, the sun's barely up and you're already parked in a rocking chair. You look like a poster child for the old folk's home."

Burns looked up and smiled. "Mornin' cowboy. Me in the old folk's home? I've got too much to do. I'll die with my boots on, Bob. When my time's up I'll know that I finished my assignment. I'll die a happy man."

"Whoa. I wasn't trying to fit you for your coffin. But everybody should retire."

"Why?"

"So they can enjoy life."

"People who can't enjoy life when they're working are just in the wrong line of work. They haven't found the right vehicle to fulfill their purpose. When you do that you don't *have* to go to work everyday, you *get* to go to work everyday. Then working doesn't seem like work. That's what it's like to be *fully engaged* — you have *enthusiasm* for your work."

"So you don't believe in retirement?"

"Not in the traditional sense."

"Do you have any idea how many times you use that phrase?" Bob asked. "I ask you a question and you say, 'Not in the traditional sense.' Don't you do *anything* in the traditional sense?"

"Not if I can help it, Bob. When I did things in the *traditional sense* I nearly went broke. The traditional sense doesn't always make the most sense. Take retirement for example. Retirement is a relatively *modern* concept that has become a *traditional* concept. When commerce was dominated by small family enterprises, grandma and grandpa gradually turned the reins over to the next generation. They slowed down a bit but didn't really 'retire.' They just took on a new role. The grandkids spent a lot of time with the grandparents who took an active hand in raising them. Mom and Dad had their hands full running the business. If you think about it, it was effective *partnership.*"

Bob thought about the many pleasant memories he had of his grandparents. Burns had described pretty much what he had experienced as a child. "It doesn't work like that anymore, Burns."

"I know and it's sad in a way. That whole process made for a better society in my opinion. When Social Security came along in the middle of the last century it gave the masses incentive to stop working at age 65. Of course, not many people lived past that age back then. But that established the notion that when you turned 65 you ought to retire."

"But Social Security," Bob was quick to point out, "went the way of the dinosaur."

"And they said it would last forever, Bob. Heck, people now days live to be a hundred. Thirty-five years is a long time to be turned out to pasture. What are you going to do with the rest of your life? You can only play so much golf and even going fishing every day gets old. Anyway, I think people should simply think of changing vehicles instead of retiring. They might consider another vocation that allows them to gear down some or become more engaged in volunteer work. The happiest old folks — as you would say, Bob — are charging just as hard as their little old bodies will let them. They enjoy life."

Bob pulled up a rocker next to Burns. "What are you reading?"

"*Stories of the Golden West* — it's a collection of Westerns written by three of my favorite authors: Louis L'Amour, Zane Grey and Max Brand."

"I know those names. I think my dad read every paperback Western that ever came off the press. He especially liked the three authors you just mentioned. I never read Westerns growing up but it's funny, after Dad died I started reading a few. I'm starting to appreciate them more as I grow older.

"You know Burns, you talking about retirement and grandparents and all makes me think. It's strange but even before the time I arrived here to do this story on you and Diamond Enterprises I've felt like I was traveling back in time. I even dreamed about home on my flight to Tulsa. I was with my grandpa and he was playing his guitar and singing like he always did when I was a kid. He was playing my favorite song, *Oklahoma Hills*."

"I remember that one, Bob. *Way down yonder in the Indian Nation...*"

"That's it. And as I was driving through the Osage, a flood of memories came over me. I guess all of that, plus my time with you here, just got me to wondering."

"You were thinking it might be nice to stay weren't you?"

"Yeah, how did you know?"

"I felt the same way when I was living in New Jersey. You'll never shake all the manure off your boots, Bob. You grew up here. These hills are a part of you. The lessons you learned growing up here have helped make you who you are."

"And that's what I was wondering about, Burns. You're such a paradox. On one hand, you're an old cowboy, stuck in the past. A romantic locked in a time capsule while the world spins away into the future. On the other, you're the most progressive business person I've ever met. You don't seem to have the need to conform to anyone else's standards. You're comfortable in your own skin. How do you do it?"

"Boy, that covers a lot of ground, Bob. When I came back here I thought all I wanted was to get back to my roots and ranch. You know, it was all about the lifestyle. Let me have my family, my cows and horses and leave me the heck alone. I thought this way of life was a birthright. But that wasn't realistic. No one can roll the clock back. I couldn't and you can't either. Thomas Wolfe was right. You can never go home again."

"But *you* did."

"But it wasn't the same home I left. It changed and I had to change too. I thought I wanted out of the rat race — to leisurely rock away here on my porch, so to speak. But that's not what I really wanted."

"So, what *did* you want?"

"I guess I really didn't know at the time. The way of life I knew here growing up wasn't the same way of life I found when I came back. Everything had changed. Trying to make a living ranching was just a struggle. I was just trying to survive. I wanted everything to change back to the way I knew it. I didn't realize it but it was me who had to change.

"Bob, this ranch is just a small part of Diamond Enterprises. It's just a vehicle, like many others, that's enabled me to fulfill my purpose of feeding a hungry world. If a vehicle no longer serves its purpose, it's time to move on. I'd hated to give up the ranch and still would — but if it were no longer a good vehicle to serve that purpose, I could let it go."

"Just like that?"

"These hills will always be a part of me just like they're a part of you. No one can take our memories away from us. I remember attending an exhibit of Norman Rockwell's art years ago. You know Rockwell was most famous for the covers he created for the Saturday Evening Post. They were all on display at this exhibit. One cover from a 1927 issue intrigued me. It featured an old cowboy sporting a Baxter Black mustache dressed out in his prairie best, wearing his hat, bandana, boots, spurs, chaps and a six-gun. He was sitting next to an old phono-graph player with a far-away look in his eyes. In his hand was a record with this title: *Dreams of Long Ago*. I can relate to that old cowboy — I'll bet you can, too."

"Wouldn't it be nice if we could turn back the clock?" Bob interrupted.

"I think you're more of a romantic than I am, Bob. We think it would be nice. But would it?"

"No, I don't suppose so. It doesn't make any difference anyway. Time is a one-way street — it only moves forward."

"And we must too. I watched an interesting documentary about the history of Western movies. It pointed out that the recurring theme of the Western is always about *moving on*. As our nation expanded westward there was always another fron-tier to explore.

"You still got that piece of paper I gave you, Bob?"

Bob reached inside his shirt pocket, unfolded it and handed it to Burns.

Burns wrote the word *Pioneer* at the 3rd base position of the diamond and handed it back to Bob. "That's the answer to your question, Bob. I *am* an old cowboy — and I'm not getting any younger. But more importantly I'm a *pioneer*. The Western is really the same story just told in different ways. It will never die — because there's always a new chapter. There are always new frontiers to conquer. I don't want to be a mere reader of history, I want to make it. I want to write the next chapter. For an organization to adapt and change it has to cultivate and promote a pioneering spirit. If you're not the lead dog, the view's always the same. I want Diamond Enterprises to be the lead dog."

Bob looked at the diamond Burns had drawn on the paper. The bases were loaded. *Purpose* was on first, *Partner* on second and *Pioneer* was at third. Home plate was empty. What would Burns put there? He was about to ask but thought better of it. Burns would reveal it in his own good time. He folded the paper and put it back in his shirt pocket.

"Bob, have you ever wondered what it is about Westerns that draw people like moths to light?"

"I guess I've never thought about it."

"I found the best answer in the forward of this book. Here, let me read it to you:

There is no other kind of American literary endeavor that has so repeatedly posed the eternal questions — how do I wish to live?, in what do I believe?, what do I want from life?, what have I to give to life? — as has the Western story.

"So, in psychological terms, the Western represents *self-actualization* — the need to fulfill our own unique potential. That's the story of the West and that's its appeal. It's not about a period in time. It's the story of life itself.

"You asked what I wanted, Bob. That was it. I didn't even know it but I wanted the answers to those questions. I found the answers when I discovered my purpose. It was the catalyst that launched Diamond Enterprises and it started me on an evolutionary path of change that has continued to this day — and the dominoes just keep falling."

U p until now, Bob thought of Burns Marcus as — to paraphrase Winston Churchill — an enigma wrapped in a riddle. On the outside, Burns was a picture of the past. On the inside, he was a picture of the future. Those two pictures were finally coming into focus for Bob. He felt like he had finally broken the code of Burns Marcus' soul. He exhibited all the traits of the hero in a Zane Grey Western. He knew how he wished to live, what he believed, what he wanted from life and what he had to give to life.

Bob was starting to really understand the man and the philosophy he had embraced to create this dynamic organization. *Dynamic* — that was a perfect description of Burns Marcus. He epitomized the very definition of dynamic — continuous change, activity and progress. He was constantly evolving. Burns Marcus wasn't a relic of a bygone era, he was a 21st Century *pioneer*. Had he lived in the 1800s he would have been running alongside the likes of Jim Bridger and Kit Carson. And they would have had to hustle to keep up with him.

Bob had been experiencing somewhat of an evolution himself in his time with Burns. He was becoming more of an admirer as opposed to a researcher of his subject. He found himself getting caught up in the story he was writing. Emotion was overtaking objectivity. But instead of fighting it he did something that surprised himself. He talked to Burns about it.

"Burns, over the course of my time with you, a funny thing has happened."

"What's that, Bob?"

"Well, as I've listened to your story I've — it's hard to explain — I've thought about *my story*."

"The story you're writing?"

"No. I mean my own *personal* story. I guess maybe I'm struggling with the questions of 'how do I wish to live, what do I believe in, what do I want from life and what have I to give to life' — the questions you said the Western novel poses."

"I can understand that. You've rekindled a lot of memories while you've been here. That gets a man to thinking."

"I guess that has something to do with it. I've got to admit that I was more than somewhat skeptical of your whole philosophy. But listening to *your* philosophy has made me analyze *my* philosophy."

Burns smiled. "Isn't skepticism mandatory in a journalist's job description?"

"I suppose. But I'm starting to buy into your concept of purposeful leadership. You've provoked me to challenge some very strongly held conceptions I've had about business — and life."

"That's good."

"And that brings me to my next question. Lots of people — and leaders — talk about change. But in the end, more is said than done. When you're a pioneer, how do you get others to join the wagon train of change?"

"You have to understand *schemas*, Bob."

"Schemas?"

"You know, like a schematic diagram. If you want to know how something is wired you look at a schematic diagram. Schema is a psychological term that describes how we human beings are wired. Schemas are formed from everything we've learned throughout our lives. Think of them as sort of like *ruts* in your brain."

"That paints a graphic picture, Burns."

"There you go. You got a picture of a rut in your mind just then. I said *rut* and your schema had a picture that corresponded with that word."

"What's that got to do with change?"

"Everything. It's hard to change because we get stuck in those ruts. And here's the bad news. Research shows that once those ruts — or schemas — are fully formed, we're *stuck* with them. That's why it's difficult to change. We're stuck in those ruts."

"So are you saying it's *impossible* to change?"

"No, it's just difficult. Research also shows that we build *new* schemas — or cut new ruts. I'll give you an example."

Bob held up his hand. "Wait a minute. I hope you're not going to drag me back down to the barn again, Burns."

"No, I'm going to let you off easy this time."

"Just a story?"

"Just a story, Bob. When I was a youngster my Dad taught me how to drive. One of the nice things about growing up around here, as you'll recall, was that there wasn't much traffic on our country roads. It was a good thing, too, because those roads were essentially one lane. I can still remember the first time I drove our old pickup after a big rain. You remember how sloppy those roads would get?"

"I sure do," Bob chuckled. "Whoever was first out on the roads after a big rain had to cut the ruts. It was slippery sledding."

"Well, you remember then, that you cut those ruts right down the middle of the road so you didn't slide into the bar ditch. But once those ruts were cut, that was the path everyone took. Stay in those ruts and you stayed out of the ditch.

"That's what I was doing, just truckin' along in those ruts. Then I faced a problem I had yet to experience in my driving lessons. Another truck was coming at me from the opposite direction. If I tried to move over I'd slide off in the ditch, but I'd have a head-on collision if I stayed in my ruts. I started to panic and asked Dad what in the world I was supposed to do. He calmly explained that country road etiquette called for me to share the ruts with the oncoming vehicle.

"He told me to slow down, ease over and put my left front wheel in the right-hand rut. That was a trick. I pulled hard to the right and finally climbed out. After fishtailing awhile I finally managed to drop my left-hand wheels into the right-hand rut. The truck approaching me from the other direction did the same thing. We passed each other without incident. I breathed a big sigh of relief. Now, you know what happened next don't you?"

"Been there, done that," Bob said. "You pulled back to the middle and settled into both ruts again."

"Yep. And boy it felt good to be back in those ruts — once again happily truckin' on down the road. You see where I'm going with this don't you, Bob?"

"We tend to slide right back into our old schemas."

"Bingo."

"So what's the solution?"

"Change is a process. Remember how I told you that most organizations tend to be either *personality-driven* or *crisis-driven?*"

"Yes."

"Well, it's easy for leaders to get stuck in their organizational ruts. A crisis is like an oncoming vehicle. It forces them out of their ruts until the crisis passes."

"Then they fall right back into their old ruts," Bob interjected.

"Until there's another crisis, Bob. But remember we can build new schemas. We can cut new ruts but it's a slow process. And there has to be a more powerful motive than a crisis if we want to make organizational change work. Let's take our country road example and tweak it a little bit.

"Imagine an organization as a bus. The driver is the leader of the organization. He asks people to get on the bus with him. But what's the obvious question people want answered before they get on the bus?"

"It would have to be, 'Where are we going?'"

"That's the question every person in every organization is subconsciously asking every day. Where are we going? But leaders of crisis-driven organizations, which are motivated by reward and punishment, don't have a very good answer. They respond with, 'Trust me, I know this road. You just get on the bus and do as you're told.' Then they go zigzagging down the road dodging the oncoming crises. That's an organization rife with anxiety. When their passengers get a chance they'll bail because the organization experiences periodic wrecks — poor financial performance and layoffs."

"So they lose money and passengers."

"Uh-huh. And the cycle continues until they crash and burn. Purposeful leaders, on the other hand, tell people what the destination is. I can tell people, 'We're off to feed a hungry world. I'm enlisting hunger fighters. If you want to join the cause, get on board.' Purpose establishes the destination. Then people *want* to get on the bus."

"Only if they buy into the purpose, Burns."

"That's why it has to be positive, powerful, simple and serving. Then people will *choose* to get on the bus rather than being *manipulated* into it by the promise of reward or the threat of punishment. They want to get on a bus that will take them on a journey that's heroic, adventurous and idealistic."

"But you'll still encounter crises."

"Yes, you will but they shouldn't *detour* you from your purpose. You have to constantly evolve and change — but it should be a matter of deciding you need to cut new ruts, instead of just dodging the next crisis."

"But even if you decide to cut new ruts what keeps you from just sliding back into your old ones?"

"Until your new ruts are as deep as the old ones you can figure on slip-sliding back and forth for awhile. Change is a process, not an event. It takes time. Just because you can't see the grass grow doesn't mean it isn't. As long as you stay focused on your purpose you can cut new ruts and stay out of the ditch. In fact, you have to continually cut new ruts.

"Change is especially difficult in an organization because you're not just dealing with one person, you've got a whole herd of people who are conditioned in old patterns of behavior. And every one of them is at a different place on the road of change. An organization should be dynamic. Change is a critical part of a purpose-driven culture. You cut new ruts and you even change and add new vehicles when necessary. You might need a new bus or even a plane or a train."

"Can you change *too much,* Burns?"

"Do you know what the fundamental principle of architectural design is, Bob?"

"If memory serves me correctly it's *form follows function.*"

"That's right. I've added another step to it and come up with my formula for organizational development. *Form follows function and function follows purpose.* Most organizations are founded with some purpose, however ambiguous it may be, in mind. They really focus more on the functions they want to perform. Then the form or structure of the organization more or less evolves to effectively perform those functions. After awhile the form becomes sacred. Preserve the form at all costs. The functions are only slightly less sacred than the form. *We've always done it this way.* Ask someone what the purpose is and they'll look at you like my banker did when I asked him to tell me what the bank's mission was. The form and functions should continually evolve to effectively serve the purpose.

"But you don't change for change's sake. There is one constant. You have to stay focused on your purpose. You can remember driving a tractor when you were growing up can't you?"

"Sure."

"If you wanted to plant a straight row what did you focus on?"

"I picked out a point at the other end of the field — a fence post or something like that — and made a beeline for that."

"And if you lost your focus what happened?"

"I zigzagged quite a bit."

"Purposeful leadership is about keeping your eye on the purpose of the organization and then pointing it out to everyone else and saying that's where we're headed — it's that fence post down at the end of the field."

"So," Bob said, "purpose is the destination. What do you do when you get there?"

"There's seedtime and harvest, Bob. Once you bring the crop in you start the process all over again. You still have that piece of paper I gave you?"

Bob smiled with anticipation. He'd been waiting for this moment. What would Burns write below home plate? He pulled the paper from his shirt pocket, unfolded it and handed it to him. It was starting to look a little ragged by now.

Burns pulled out his pen and started writing but nothing appeared on the page. "Dang it, it's out of ink. Well, I'll go get a pen out of the house."

Bob couldn't stand the suspense. "Here use mine," he said, pulling out his pen and fumbling to get the cap off. He thrust it into Burns's hand.

"Thank you, Bob."

Burns appeared to be in no hurry. Bob was like a kid eyeing presents under the tree on Christmas morning. He looked eagerly over Burns's shoulder.

Finally Burns wrote something below home plate on the diamond — *Profit.*

"I knew it!" Bob blurted out. "I knew you'd get around to talking about making money. You're a *capitalist* after all."

Burns looked amused. "Did I ever say I wasn't?"

"No, but I've been with you here the better part of a week and you've spent most of the time talking about things that have *nothing* to do with the bottom line."

"Bob, *everything* I've talked about has to do with the bottom line. I'm an *unashamed* capitalist. You just have to put profit in its proper perspective."

"What do you mean?"

"You can't effectively serve a customer without engaging in free enterprise. It's like the invisible hand that economist Adam Smith talked about. You serve yourself by serving others. It's the great paradox.

"Financial success, or *profit*, is the byproduct of purpose, partnering and pioneering. You have to touch all the bases, Bob. It all begins with *Purpose*. You have to *Partner* with people if you want to accomplish anything of greatness. You have to foster a *Pioneer* spirit to successfully adapt and change. *Profit* is the fuel that feeds an organization. It enables us to continue fulfilling our purpose of feeding a hungry world. *And that's the bottom line.*"

XII

Burns Marcus answered every one of Bob's questions with a metaphor. He talked about horses, trucks, tractors, busses and baseball. But sprinkled in between the ruts and roping were twenty-four carat jewels of wisdom. Like most of the old farmers and ranchers Bob knew when he was growing up, Burns was a student of the world around him. These old sages looked at the sky and could tell you if and when it was going to rain. The land and the livestock told them if it was going to be a hard winter or an early spring. The thing that made Burns different was that his sixth sense extended to the highest rung of the taxonomical hierarchy — he knew people.

The morning had disappeared as quickly as the dew under the bright summer sun. Burns, Jane and Bob had lunch. Today was different though. Instead of whisking Bob away for another experiential object lesson on the ranch, Burns seemed content to sit on the porch and visit. He knew his time with Bob was soon coming to an end and it was as if he had some things he wanted to make sure were said before he got away. Now it was Burns, not Bob, who drove the conversation.

"Bob, you said something this morning that I want to ask you about."

"What's that?"

"You said *my story* made you think about *your story*."

"That's right."

"Tell me more about that."

"You sound like — who was it you said — Dr. Phil?"

Burns laughed. "I'm no psychologist."

"Maybe you are. You just have a unique method of therapy."

"What do you mean?"

"Well, you don't just answer my questions. You tell a story and then make a point. You never just come out and say, 'Here's the way it is.' Why?"

"I think you answered your own question."

"*I did?* I must have missed it."

"You said *my story* made you think about *your story*."

"I don't get it."

"Remember our lesson on schemas?"

"You mean *ruts*."

"That's right, ruts. You may not remember schema. But you'll remember those ruts won't you?"

Bob nodded. "When you talked about your Dad teaching you to drive on those muddy roads, I was right there with you."

"That's because you had experienced the same thing. Your childhood driving experiences were firmly etched in your schemas. You had a picture in your mind's eye that matched up pretty close with the picture I presented you with — the picture of my driving experience."

"It was more than that. It was a video — a flashback in living color."

"See, your answer is even telling. You used the words *video* and *living color*," Burns snorted. "Those are 20th Century terms, Bob. Kids today would say *virtual reality*. What I used to call a picture show or you call a video is now a *virtual reality interactive experience*."

"But virtual reality was science fiction when I was a kid."

"I know. And that's my point. Your *video* schema is more ingrained than your *virtual reality* schema. *See* what I mean?" Burns pointed to his eyes.

"Yeah," Bob smiled and nodded his head. "I do *see* what you mean."

"I can tell you something and you'll hear what I say but you may not see what I see. If you hear but don't see, odds are you'll miss the point."

"So you tell a story and make a point."

"It would be more accurate to say I tell a story *to make a point.*"

"Where did you learn that?"

"The Bible."

"The Bible?"

"Parables to be more specific. Parables are just stories. Stories that illustrate a lesson. Jesus told stories about fishing and farming mostly. You know why, Bob?"

"Probably because most people were engaged in those vocations or did business with someone who was."

"Yes, and everything associated with fishing and farming was indelibly etched in their schemas. The masses may not have been able to read or write but they could all see their story in his stories."

"I really do *see* what you mean. That's kind of what I've experienced talking with you the last few days. Hearing your story — and all the stories that make up your story — has got me to thinking about a lot of things."

"I'll play the part of Dr. Phil again. Talk about those things."

"I guess I came here to write a story. The fact that it brought me back to the Osage made it intriguing but I didn't realize the effect it would have on me. I've relived my youth in the process of interviewing you.

"Most of my assignments give me a certain level of access to the subjects. But you've almost taken me to raise this week — I never thought I'd be ridin' and ropin'."

"Stick around and I'll have you building fence."

"Building fence — I don't think so. You seem to be getting rid of fences — at least the barbed wire variety. Talk about old schemas. That's like me talking about videos in living color."

"Yeah, but I'll bet you remember how to drive T-posts and string wire. You might even be old enough to remember how to actually *dig* postholes or build a rock corner."

"Rock corners — I thought about those when I drove through your entrance."

"Uh, I didn't mean to get you off track, Bob. You were saying…"

"Well, Burns, I don't want to overstep my bounds. But I see more than an article here."

"What do you mean?"

"A lot of people, a lot of organizations and a lot of the leaders in those organizations need to hear the story of Diamond Enterprises. It needs to be a book."

"And you want to write it?"

"Now, don't misunderstand me. I'd love to write it but I don't want you to think I'm just trying to cash in on my good fortune of landing the assignment to write this article. I really believe…" Bob's voice trailed off.

"Believe what?"

"I believe that the world needs purposeful people, purposeful leaders and purpose-driven organizations."

"I do too, Bob. *And that's why you're here.*"

"Well, I wouldn't say *that* but…"

"But nothing," Burns interrupted. "That first morning you showed up you said I couldn't run under the radar forever, Bob. And you were right. Have you ever wondered why there has been so little written about Diamond or me? I'm pretty picky about who I'll trust with the telling of my story because I want them to get it right. I don't want to be the CEO flavor of the month only to see a bunch of people give lip service to the philosophy that built this organization.

"I've been doing research on writers for several years now. I sorted through the usual suspects but I picked you out of the lineup a long time ago. I've read everything you've ever written. I want you to write our story, Bob. I want you to write a book about the *power of purposeful leadership.*"

Bob sat motionless. No words passed between the two men for a moment.

"I'm not here by luck of the draw?"

"I refused to be interviewed by the other writers the publisher suggested. When she finally pitched you, I said OK."

"So you've really been interviewing me instead of me interviewing you?"

"Let's just say we've been interviewing each other."

"OK. But why me?"

"I could give you a lot of reasons. First you had the right pedigree. Having grown up on a ranch here in the Osage, I knew you had common sense. Next, you've written a lot about business and leadership. I didn't always agree with the point of view of the people you wrote about but that wasn't your doing. You were simply writing about their approaches and philosophies but that gives you a basis to benchmark my ideas against. And you've validated that by some of the questions you've posed. I might add that you haven't been an easy sell. You approached this assignment with a healthy dose of skepticism. All of those things were in your favor — but there was one other thing that tipped the scales."

"What's that?"

"It's hard to describe but most writers only go about one layer deep. They present the facts but sometimes I feel like there's more to be told. Bob, you have a unique ability to see the story behind the story — and tell it in a way that makes a person feel it instead of just reading it."

Bob felt humbled and proud at the same time. Burns described his writing style better than he could have himself.

"I have to ask you this. If you knew all of this before I got this assignment then why didn't you just contact me about writing your book?"

Burns leaned back and started rocking.

"Oh, I wanted to look you eyeball to eyeball and size you up from close up. I was looking for a clue that might confirm what I thought to be true about you."

"Did you find it?"

"Yep."

"Well? What was it?"

"It happened this morning. When you came out on the porch and said — how did you say it — something about how *my story* made you think about *your story*. That told me that you got it. If you could get inside my skin to where you could feel what I feel then you can tell *my* story.

"There's just one more thing I want you to do before we get down to forming our partnership."

"Partnership?"

"How quickly you forget, Bob. Remember, we operate on the partnership principle around here. We've got to sit down and work out the details."

"And what's the *one* more thing you want me to do?"

B ob looked around and sized up the other people in the room. He felt a little like the new kid in class and in a way he was. He was the only person here who wasn't a member of the Diamond Enterprises family. Well, maybe he *was* part of the family. He was going to be *partnering* with Burns Marcus on his book.

This was the "one more thing" that Burns wanted him to do. When new partners joined Diamond Enterprises they were enrolled in *Cowboy Boot Camp*. The CBC, in Burns's words, "started partners on the path of building a 'purpose-based schema.'"

Bob was startled back to the moment by the sharp ringing of a bell — a *cowbell*. On the business end of the bell was a red-headed woman who was having way too much fun bringing the meeting to order. Some of the participants got into the act by responding with some good natured "mooing." Burns may have created a purpose-driven culture at Diamond Enterprises but it was a culture flavored with a heavy dose of cowboy seasoning. He may have been a romantic but he figured out that the world needed a good dose of romanticism and turned what his history professor perceived as a negative into a positive. Cowboy was *cool* at Diamond Enterprises.

"All right, y'all, let's head 'em up and move 'em out. My name is Sally and I'm in charge of this rodeo." The room grew quiet. "To kick things off I want to introduce you to our partner-in-chief and head hunger fighter, Burns Marcus."

Burns Marcus emerged from the back of the room to polite applause. Bob hadn't even noticed Burns being in the room. He must have slipped in just before the meeting started.

"Thank you, Sally, and I want to thank each of you for being here today. What you'll be participating in over the next several days is what I consider to be one of the most critical steps in solidifying our partnership with you.

"We're going to do some puzzle building. Each of us holds a critical piece of that puzzle and it's important that we all find out where and how our piece fits into the Diamond Enterprises picture.

"The most important word in the Diamond vocabulary is purpose. You're going to hear it a lot. Not just this week but for as long as we partner. Purpose is the glue that holds our partnership together.

"Our purpose here at Diamond is 'to feed a hungry world.' We exist for that purpose. Now, you're going to learn about all the vehicles we use to fulfill that purpose. But I want you to know that there is more to feeding a hungry world than meets the stomach.

"We're not here just to feed the human body. We're here to feed the human spirit. Each of us was put here on earth for a purpose. This morning I'm going to share how I discovered my purpose and how that discovery led to the founding of Diamond Enterprises."

Another layer of the onion was being peeled. But Bob wasn't doing the peeling. Burns Marcus was Over the next hour or so he shared much with the group that Bob had just heard in his visits with Burns at the ranch. As Bob surveyed the faces of those sitting around him it was obvious that Burns Marcus had an unusual ability to connect with people at a level that transcended the physical. The man was genuine. There was nothing phony about him. This wasn't an ego trip or an exercise in manipulation. He was there for the people in that room — not the other way around.

"To conclude my part of the program today I want you to know that it's not enough for you to know what our purpose is. You have to buy into it. You have to live it and breathe it. And to do that you have to know what *your* piece of the puzzle is and how it fits into that purpose. Because we only reach our full potential as an organization by helping you reach your full potential as an individual. I'll be dropping in on you over the next few days so we can get better acquainted."

The applause this time was enthusiastic. Burns exited the room with little fanfare. The Cowboy Boot Camp had begun.

The Cowboy Boot Camp was conducted at a lodge nestled among the wooded hills of Persimmon Ridge right on the southeastern tip of Osage County. On Holmes Peak immediately to the north stood *The American*, the 21-story-tall Indian warrior. To the south was a beautiful view of downtown Tulsa. In between was the Gilcrease Museum which housed the largest collection of Western art in the world. Several outdoor activities were incorporated into the CBC, allowing participants to enjoy the inspirational setting steeped in the rich history of the Oklahoma Hills.

Bob was assigned to a team of three as were all the participants. He became well acquainted with his teammates, learning where they came from and what led them to Diamond Enterprises. It was obvious that anybody who found themselves here had been through an extensive qualifying process. It made Bob think about how thoroughly Burns had researched him. He was learning that not everyone was a candidate for Diamond's purpose-driven culture. They had to be at a point in their lives where they were ready to be *intrinsically* motivated. That, Bob discovered, wasn't necessarily a function of age, background, ethnicity, gender, experience or education. Different people reach that point at different stages of their lives — and some may not get to that point at all. Sometimes the reward and punishment conditioning is more powerful than the individual's desire to choose, in the words of Robert Frost, "the road less traveled by."

Over the next several days the participants went through a series of exercises that forced them to dig deep inside of themselves. Bob was in the unusual position of being an observer *and* a participant in the process. He started out wearing his observer hat. He was, after all, a writer conducting research for an article that now was taking on new life as a book. But as the week wore on, he experienced a mind-set metamorphosis. Yes, he was learning all about Diamond Enterprises and their purpose-driven culture, but he discovered that he was learning a lot about himself. The boot camp forced Bob to deal with those eternal questions Burns talked about. How do I wish to live? In what do I believe? What do I want from life? What have I to give to life? Bob was becoming *engaged* in the process.

That process made Bob think about Burns working his way through the professional provoker's book. Like all CBC participants, he completed assessments that helped him identify his natural strengths and talents. He learned that *his piece of the puzzle* was imprinted with a unique behavioral pattern. Bob was *not* surprised to discover that he was a natural born communicator. Writing was a perfect vehicle for him. He *was* surprised to find there were skills he needed to enhance to be more effective and with the help of Sally he put together a development plan. On one hand it bothered him to think that he was not maximizing his talents. On the other, he felt good about the fact that he was now engaged in a process to help him on the path of reaching his full potential.

On the last day of Cowboy Boot Camp, Bob noticed an older man sitting in the back of the room. He knew he wasn't a participant because this was the first day he had seen him. He seemed familiar but Bob couldn't place him. He could have passed for Burns Marcus's brother — he looked like another old cowboy, dressed in jeans and boots. Curiosity got the best of Bob. During the break he walked up to the man and said, "I ought to know you but I just can't remember from where."

The older man smiled. "Well, I know you, Bob."

"You do?" Bob was embarrassed that he couldn't recall the man's name.

"Sure. Burns has told me all about you."

Bob now realized he had never met the man but he had seen his picture. But where? It wasn't a recent picture — it had been taken when the man was much younger. The light bulb went on in Bob's memory bank. "You're the *professional provoker*! I saw your picture on the back of Burns's book."

"You can just call me J.F. And that was the back of *my* book. It was just Burns's copy."

"It was twenty-five years ago when Burns said he heard you speak. I never thought about actually meeting you. I figured you were dead."

"Well, Bob, as Mark Twain would say, 'the reports of my death have been greatly exaggerated.' I may be *over* the hill but I'm not *buried* there — yet."

"What are *you* doing here?"

"Oh, I drop in on these Cowboy Boot Camps periodically — just to meet some of the new partners and to evaluate the process."

"So *you* work for Diamond?"

"Oh, you could say that. A better way to put it would be to say that I'm a…"

"*Partner*." Bob couldn't restrain himself from finishing the sentence. He had heard the word *partner* so much the last several days that it came out of his mouth automatically.

"You're catching on, Bob."

"I came here to write an article about Burns and…"

"Now, you're going to write his book. Shall we continue finishing each other's sentences?"

"Maybe that's a sign of a good partnership, J.F."

"I think I'm going to like you, Bob. You kind of remind me of me."

"Then why don't we get better acquainted? I'd like to spend a little time with the man who *provoked* Burns Marcus to change his ways."

"What do you mean?"

"He credits you with being the catalyst that started him on the path of purposeful leadership."

"Oh, you mean when he heard me speak at the convention in San Antonio."

"That, and your book. He says it transformed his life."

"That seems like a million years ago."

"It was just twenty-five."

"When you're as old as I am it just seems like a million. There's a lot more to the story than the convention and the book. Did Burns tell you that?"

"No. I'd like to hear about it though. I mean I'm going to *have* to hear about it if I'm going to write this book. But I'm enlisted in Cowboy Boot Camp for the rest of the day. And tomorrow I'm heading home."

"Here's my card. Stop by and see me before you take off."

Bob looked at J.F.'s card. Right underneath his name was the most unusual title Bob had ever seen on a business card — *Professional Provoker*.

Bob feared that Burns, and Thomas Wolfe, may have been right. Maybe you can never go home again. But you can always go back for a visit. And Bob's trip back to the Osage turned out to be way more than he had bargained for. He had come to write an article about Burns Marcus and Diamond Enterprises and was walking away with a book deal. And not just any book — a book that would define his career as a writer. Look out *New York Times Best Seller List*. Here comes Bob Fooshee.

He was just trying to catch his breath now — and catch a train. Instead of flying he was booked on the *Great Plains Flyer* — one of the new bullet trains that ran on the *Coast–To-Coast Railway System*. But he had one more stop to make before he headed to the depot in Tulsa. He looked at the business card and double checked the address. He smiled and shook his head — what kind of a character would actually describe himself as a *professional provoker*? Bob was about to find out. He looked for the door bell but what he found instead was a spur that had been converted into a doorknocker. He grabbed the shank of the spur and gave it a couple of good raps. The door opened.

"Hello J.F., I like your doorknocker."

"I hung up my spurs years ago and decided to turn one of them into this doorknocker, Bob. It makes a good conversation piece and it's a reminder of what I used to do in another life. Come on in."

"So, you're an old cowboy, too?"

"I am indeed. I understand you are as well. In fact, Sandy told me you put on quite a bronc riding exhibition out at the ranch the other day and that you're not a bad hand with a rope either."

Bob blushed. "News travels fast around here doesn't it?"

"You've made quite an impression. Have a chair. I've got the coffee pot on. Are you ready for 'the rest of the story' as Paul Harvey used to say?"

"Burns used that same phrase the other day. Who is this Paul Harvey anyway?"

"Oh, he used to be on the radio years ago. He had a program called *The Rest of the Story.*"

"Oh yeah, I can remember my dad listening to that on the radio in our pickup. Anyway, I just assumed that your role in the saga of Burns Marcus and Diamond Enterprises ended after Burns worked his way through your book. He never said anything about you two actually getting acquainted. I didn't realize you were located here in Tulsa. It's ironic that you all were separated by eighty miles and the first time you met was in San Antonio."

"We actually didn't meet in San Antonio. He just heard me speak there."

"Oh, that's right. And that's where he bought your book. So when *did* you meet?"

"A year later."

"Where?"

"At the cattlemen's convention in Denver."

"You must have been their resident speaker."

J.F. laughed. "Well, you don't find many management consultants with degrees in animal science who actually cowboyed for a living. I've worked with all kinds of organizations in all kinds of industries but my background gave me a strategic advantage when it came to agribusiness."

"So you were a management consultant?"

"Still am. You just keep trying to bury me don't you, Bob?"

"Your card says you're a professional provoker."

"And my wife will tell you that I'm really good at it, too. But that's what good management consultants do. They provoke people to think about what they do and why they do it. And if need be, they provoke them to change."

"And most of us need to change?"

"Only people who want to be successful."

"So tell me how you and Burns met."

"Burns walked up to me before my presentation in Denver and said, 'I heard you speak in San Antonio last year. And I have to tell that I thought you were the worst speaker I had ever heard.'"

"I'll bet that made your day. What'd you say?"

"I didn't say anything. I was left speechless. And that's a terrible thing to happen to someone who makes a big part of his living talking. But then he goes on to tell me about buying my book, discovering his purpose and how that started him on a different path in life."

"Then what happened?"

"It was time for the program to start. So our first conversation was pretty short. But that was the beginning of a relationship that has lasted to this day. And the program that day was what really provoked Burns to think about what kind of an organization he wanted to build."

"So you provoked him again. That's twice in twelve months. What'd you say to get him going this time?"

"It's not what I said. It's what Burns and everyone else in the audience said."

"I don't get it. I thought *you* were the speaker."

"Let me try to put what we did that day into context for you. The early part of this century was a time of rapid consolidation in many industries. Retailing was dominated by Wal-Mart. Microsoft was king of the technology mountain. Some thought the big would eat the little. But that wasn't necessarily the case. It was really a time that might best be described as a *realignment* of industries. For example, the major airlines, or the legacy carriers as they were called, were going belly up. Regional carriers like Southwest had developed successful business models and when the industry was deregulated they started dominating the skies.

"Trade associations were experiencing this realignment too — especially those whose members included small and intermediate sized businesses. So these associations were struggling to keep up with the times and help their members adapt. The food industry was no exception. And the beef industry was an integral part of the food industry. So I was at this convention to help them figure out the direction their association needed to take for the future."

"And how did you do that?"

"I had developed a very simple but effective way to involve their membership in the process. In a general session, I asked their members four questions:

- Look back 30 years ago and describe what the world and your industry looked like. What changes have taken place that you have experienced in those 30 years?

- Now look 30 years into the future and describe what the world and your industry *will* look like. What changes will take place in the next 30 years?

- What will you, as an individual, have to do to be a part of the future you just described?

- What will your association have to do to help you be part of that future?"

Bob sat back in his chair. "Sounds like a simplified strategic planning process."

"That's exactly what it is. I'm a great believer in simple. It's not the whole process I used but it was a way I *provoked* organizations to think about the future."

"How did you pull that off in a general session? I mean there had to be hundreds of people in that room."

"That's right. We put people in small teams at round tables. Each team recorded their answers. We revealed the questions one at a time and after each question we debriefed with the group at large."

"Didn't it get a little chaotic?"

"Not at all. We turned it into a big talk show. I played the role of talk show host and facilitated the process while association staffers armed with microphones roamed the crowd. That enabled the teams to share answers where everyone could hear. Cameras focused on whoever was speaking and several big screens let everyone see the whole thing."

"OK, but where did the 30 year thing come from? I mean most strategic planners ask people to look three to five years into the future."

"Can you remember five years ago, Bob?"

"Sure."

"Does it seem like a long time ago?"

"Seems like yesterday."

"And five years in the future will go just as quickly. If you ask people to look five years into the future they'll simply see it as an extension of the present and they see the present as merely an extension of the past. When we look 30 years ahead we tend to do a better job of identifying the changes we'll really need to make."

"All right, I buy that. But why would you ask people to look 30 years into the past?"

"It's a lot easier to look at the past and identify the changes they've *already* experienced. It helps them understand that they have experienced a *lot* of changes in the past 30 years — and survived. And it kind of primes the pump for looking at the future. It also helps them see they'd better tighten their cinches and get ready to ride. Change just picks up speed in the future."

"What was the result?"

"I've facilitated this process many times in my life, Bob. I tell people to describe the future as they think it really *will* be instead of like they *hope* it will be. And there's one thing I can always count on. The participants basically describe the future exactly alike. I'm always fascinated by how futuristic they are in their answers. And they all agree on what they as individuals and their organization, or in this case their association, will have to do to be a part of the future they described.

"So," Bob mused, "it really gets down to being a question of being willing to do what they just said they *must do* to be part of the future they just described."

"That's the bottom line. I'll never forget what happened in that particular session. One guy stood up and grabbed a microphone. 'Well, that may be what the future is going to be like,' he announced. 'But I'll be damned if I'm going to be part of it!'"

Bob laughed. "Sounds like you *really* provoked him."

"Yeah, I guess I did. But he inadvertently made an excellent point. It's one thing to agree on what we must do to succeed in the future but it's quite another to make the decision to do it."

"And another to *actually* do it," Bob added.

"Yes, it is. You have to be motivated to change. And in my experience not many people or organizations have the *motivation* to get it done."

"Why?"

"Because far too many are motivated primarily by reward and punishment. They're just trying to survive."

"Why did I know you were going to say that?"

"Probably because you've been hanging around Burns Marcus. Burns had the right motivation."

"Purpose."

"That's right. After the session he came up to me and told me what had happened in his life over the past year. He understood that if you're just trying to survive you'll fail. Burns was focused on serving. He had discovered his purpose and was intrinsically motivated. But he made a quantum leap during our visioning session that day. He saw that the key to the future was to partner with other people to do what they couldn't do by themselves.

"And that was the beginning of *our* partnership."

Talking with J.F. was giving Bob a completely different perspective on his story. His time with Burns let him get inside the skin of the founder of Diamond Enterprises. He knew what made Burns Marcus tick. His time with J.F. was helping him understand how Burns Marcus was able to take his purpose as a person and turn it into a movement — a cause that was bigger than one person.

"J.F., I've spent enough time around Burns to hear the word *partner* about a thousand times."

"Only slightly fewer times than the word *purpose,* I imagine."

"You got that right. So, tell me about *your* partnership with Burns."

"I started working with Burns as a consultant. Right away I knew that working with Burns was not only going to be fun but that he was going to get things done. He was serious. He didn't have the time or money to play games. Some clients want you to tell them what they want to hear. I never lasted long with clients like that. I have a bad habit of telling people what they *need* to hear."

"I'd say that's a good habit."

"That's exactly what Burns said. He took the visioning session to heart and asked me what kind of an organization I thought it would take to succeed in the future."

"What kind of organization *did* you think it would take?"

"Diamond Enterprises."

"I don't understand. Diamond Enterprises didn't exist back then."

"It did — but just in my mind's eye. Oh, it didn't have a name. And it didn't even have a product or service to sell. It was a concept, an ideal."

"So how did you conceive of this *ideal* organization?"

"It was the result of a combination of things. I knew from my experience of working for a couple of major corporations what didn't work. So, I backed into it."

"How?"

"It all started when I discovered *my* purpose."

"Oh boy, here we go again. And what's *your* purpose?"

"To help people reach their full potential."

"OK, who *provoked* you?"

J.F. walked over to his desk and returned with a book. "Here, you can read about it." He handed the book to Bob.

Bob recognized it as the same book Burns had shown him back at the ranch, although this copy was new. "Looks like you updated your picture. I'd recognize you right away from this one."

"You'll recognize some of what you read in there, too."

"I will?"

"Much of what you experienced at the Cowboy Boot Camp is based on that book."

"You know," Bob said, "as I was working through the exercises there it reminded me of some of what Burns told me about working through the exercises in your book. So you helped him develop the boot camp?"

"As I said, Burns was serious. He told me that he wanted to take the principles he read in that book and use them to build an organization. That's when I knew I was dealing with a man after my own heart. I wanted to do the same thing. In fact, I had been using a purpose-based approach to organizational development with clients but with mixed results."

"What was the problem?"

"Most organizations have a lot of years invested in their current cultures. The older an organization is, the more ingrained the culture."

"But if they hired you as a consultant then that means they bought into your philosophy, right?"

"Yes, but you have to understand, Bob, old schemas die hard."

"Oh, I know all about schemas. I got a schema lesson from Burns and then heard about it all over again at Cowboy Boot Camp."

"Well, an organization's culture is like a collective schema. Change for an individual is tough enough. Change for an organization is compounded by the age of the organization and the number of people who make it up."

"Can it be done?"

"Sure. But it takes time and money, two things most organizations like to invest into more tangible things like concrete and steel. They don't like to invest time and money into things that aren't tangible — what they typically call the *soft* side of their business."

"People."

"Yep. Interesting isn't it? They talk about people being their most valuable asset and I think they really believe that —

or at least they really *think* they believe that. But they don't always want to spend much time and money *developing* their most valuable asset. It's hard to teach old humans new tricks. The *spirit* may be willing but the *flesh* is weak."

"That's because we're animals, J.F."

"That's right," J.F. smiled. "But remember our animal bodies..."

"House the human spirit," Bob added with grin. "I've got that part memorized. So, working with Burns gave you a chance to build a purpose-driven culture from scratch."

"We were like two mad scientists turned loose in a human laboratory. We shared a common background — a couple of old cowboys who had done the corporate gig and thought we could do it better. We shared a common bond — we were both purpose-driven people. Diamond Enterprises provided us with a common purpose. We would be able to multiply that philosophy by building a purpose-driven organization. So we rolled up our sleeves and went to work."

"And presto, the result is the Diamond Enterprises the world knows today."

"I wish it were as easy as waving a magic wand, Bob. The reality is that it's been twenty-five years of trial, error, blood, sweat and even a tear or two. But man, it's been fun."

Bob thought back to when he first met Burns. He almost used the same words as J.F. He said it had been fun.

"J.F., how can you describe something as being so difficult and yet say it was fun?"

"Bob, we humans think we want life to be comfortable. We've been conditioned to believe it. But that's not what we really want."

"We don't?"

"Did you play sports?"

"Yes." Bob was starting to feel déjà vu all over again. J.F. talked a lot like Burns. He knew he was in for another philosophical parable.

"Think about everything you put into preparing for a game — the endless hours of conditioning and all of the practice. Do you remember what that was like?"

"Yeah, it was about like what you just said — trial, error, blood, sweat and some tears."

"Do you remember what it was like to win a big game?"

"Elation."

"But there is no elation without everything you experienced to get to that point. It wasn't just fun to win. What made it fun?"

"Knowing that you challenged yourself — and that you met the challenge."

"And once the game was over what did you do?"

"Went back to work — more trial, error, blood, sweat and tears."

"That's the human experience, Bob. Peaks and valleys, good and bad, pain and pleasure. It's all just reward and punishment if it's not for a purpose. You can persevere when you're on purpose. You can enjoy the journey when you know the destination is worthy of the trials you experience along the path. Purpose is what makes it fun.

"What makes it fun is to think about the millions of people who are positively impacted by Diamond's purpose. We're feeding a hungry world. Not just their bodies but their spirits.

"Take the Cowboy Boot Camp. All of Diamond's partners have the opportunity to find their purpose and see how it fits into that big picture of feeding a hungry world."

Bob had a look on his face that said, "I'm not completely sold."

"That's great for people who come to work for Diamond or one of their strategic partners like you. I don't mean to downplay that, J.F. but let's be realistic — Diamond can feed millions of bodies but they're not doing anything for the *spirits* of people not directly connected with Diamond."

"Oh, but they are."

"How?"

"Burns Marcus puts his money where his mouth is. We founded a nonprofit organization that makes what you experienced in the Cowboy Boot Camp available for the general public. It also takes the *purpose process* into schools, prisons and other organizations that serve people in need. Diamond Enterprises and Burns Marcus are the largest contributors. Which reminds me of a question I wanted to ask you."

"Shoot."

"What did you think about the Cowboy Boot Camp?"

"If I hadn't approached it as part of my research for the article and the book, I wouldn't have been able to muster much enthusiasm for it."

"So, from a personal point of view it was a waste of time?"

"No, I didn't say that. It took me awhile to warm up to it. But once I traded my writer hat for a participant hat I started getting into it."

"What'd you learn?"

"A lot more about Diamond. It filled in a lot of the gaps that I needed to close after my interview with Burns."

"Anything else?"

"I learned a lot about me. The process made me really examine my life. The feedback I received from my team members gave me insights that I had never thought of."

"Did you discover *your* purpose?"

Bob looked down at the floor. "No, I didn't — I feel like I flunked the class."

"Oh, I wouldn't worry about that, Bob. It's not a pass-or-fail deal. It's a process. It'll come to you."

"You reckon?"

J.F. nodded his head. "Remember, Bob. Your purpose isn't something you define — it's something you *find*. You already possess it — you just haven't found it yet."

The *Great Plains Flyer* lived up to its name. At speeds approaching 400 mph the scenery along the right-of-way looked like a continuous mural of impressionist art — a blur of green grass and blue sky punctuated by barely distinguishable man-made structures and various species of the animal kingdom. Bob was on his way *back* to Oklahoma. It had been two years since he had first met Burns Marcus on his ranch and started the odyssey that culminated in the completion of the book.

Bob knocked out his article in a matter of days after returning from his trip to Oklahoma two years earlier. Then he settled in to write the book. Bob was a bit old-fashioned when it came to writing. He preferred to peck away at a keyboard instead of just talking to his computer. It might take him a little longer to write the first draft than some of his contemporaries who used voice recognition word processing but Bob's manuscripts required little editing.

His article on Burns and Diamond Enterprises created a buzz. This both pleased Bob and made him anxious at the same time. Talk of the book started making the rounds and the success of his article created high expectations. He wanted to complete the manuscript quickly but even more importantly, he wanted to get it right.

Bob and his publisher considered many titles including *I Did It On Purpose: How Burns Marcus Built Diamond Enterprises.* When they pitched that idea to Burns he just about threw a shoe. He wouldn't hear of it. His exact words were, "I didn't build Diamond Enterprises, I was just the catalyst. It was built by all of the people who have partnered with me. *We* built Diamond Enterprises *to feed a hungry world.*" The light bulb came on when Bob heard that. The title should be *We Did It On Purpose.* Burns agreed.

Electronic media was more popular but people still bought books in hard copy. There's something about a book that has a sense of timelessness. A copy of *Tom Sawyer* today looks pretty much the same as one that came off the press in the 19th century — and it's still just as relevant. Maybe it's comforting to know that a book is always waiting for you on your bookshelf — like a good friend. And what could be more personal than a copy of a book that is personally inscribed by the author? Now that the book had been published, Bob was doing a promotional tour, interviews and book signings. The first stop was Tulsa.

Burns was throwing a big shindig at the ranch to launch the tour and celebrate. It was a day-long affair that included tours of the ranch and facilities and interviews with Bob, Burns and other long-time partners. One of the media favorites turned out to be Sandy who made a point of telling how Bob had put on a bronc riding exhibition on old Buck.

A barbeque and dance completed the agenda. Bob mingled with the media and the many Diamond partners Bob had become acquainted with over the last couple of years. He was visiting with some of his teammates from the Cowboy Boot Camp when he felt a tap on his shoulder.

"Can I have this dance cowboy?"

Sandy had traded in her boots and jeans for a dress that seemed to transform her.

"I beg your pardon, ma'am. I don't believe I know you and my mother warned me about talking to strangers."

"I don't see your momma anywhere here tonight."

"Well, maybe just this one time. But I'm warning you, keep your hands where I can see them."

Sandy took Bob's left hand with her right and slipped her left arm around his waist. "You can keep your eye on my right hand and I'll just make sure you can *feel* my left."

Right now all Bob could feel was the blood filling his face. "Whatever you say. After all you are the foreman. Or is it fore-woman?"

"You can just call me *boss*."

Bob and Sandy danced as the band played an old Bob Wills favorite, *Faded Love*.

> *As I look at the letters that you wrote to me*
> *It's you that I am thinking of*
> *As I read the lines that to me were so sweet*
> *I remember our faded love*

He may have been a native Texan but Bob Wills was an Oklahoma institution. Bob and his Texas Playboys made their mark broadcasting live from Cain's Ballroom in Tulsa during the 1930s. Since these broadcasts were carried by the 50,000 watt radio station KVOO, fans tuned in from all across the nation making Bob Wills the *King of Western Swing*. At the same time a little-known announcer was launching his career at KVOO — a young upstart by the name of Paul Harvey. And now *you know* the rest of the story.

Faded Love — the song brought back memories for Bob — memories of his grandpa. Once again he was caught in his time warp. Grandpa had grown up listening to Bob Wills on the radio and he played many of those tunes for little Bobby on those blissful summer evenings — *San Antonio Rose, Take Me Back to Tulsa, Cotton-Eyed Joe* and, of course, *Faded Love*. Bob closed his eyes and listened. He could still hear grandpa singing.

117

I miss you, Darling, more and more every day
As heaven would miss the stars above
With every heartbeat, I still think of you
And remember our faded love

Sandy whispered in Bob's ear. "Bobby."

"Uh-huh."

She was more emphatic. "Bob!"

"Yes?"

"The music's stopped."

"Not for me."

"We're the only ones on the floor."

Bob opened his eyes. "Why'd you call me *Bobby*?"

"I didn't call you Bobby. You must be dreaming. Or you've been over-served."

"Who cares? Let's keep dancing."

"On one condition."

"And that would be?"

"That we only dance *while* the band is *playing*."

"You're the boss, boss."

Bob had often thought of Sandy the last two years. On one of his trips back to visit with Burns, Sandy had coerced him into helping her move cattle. That reunited him with old Buck. Being back in the saddle again, and being with Sandy, made him think about Thomas Wolfe and Burns. Bob was thinking about going home again.

As a writer, Bob could pitch his tent and ply his trade anywhere he pleased. And each trip to the Osage made him think he might want to pitch his tent somewhere around here. He'd have to talk to Burns about that. Burns... Where was Burns? Bob hadn't seen him all day.

"Sandy, have you seen Burns?"

"You mean recently?"

"I mean tonight."

"I talked with him earlier. He said he needed to park for awhile and was going up to the house and sit on the porch."

"I've got to talk to him. Will you excuse me?"

"Sure. I think I'll call it a night anyway. I've got to ship some steers early in the morning. Want to help?"

"Do I get to ride old Buck?"

"If you can, Bob, if you can."

"You'll never let me live that day down will you? What time?"

"Be at the barn at 5:30."

"Now, I remember why I became a writer. The hours are way better than cowboyin'." Bob pulled Sandy in close to him and said good night — without uttering a word. And with that he turned and walked away.

"I'll be there," he said over his shoulder.

Sandy stared after him. "Well, I *hope* so..."

Bob was afoot so he hiked up the hill to Burns's house. It was only about a quarter of a mile. The dew was on the grass and he could almost taste the damp evening air. The music faded into the night but *Faded Love* was still playing in Bob's mind.

> *I think of the past and all the pleasures*
> *As I watch the mating of the dove*
> *It was in the springtime that you said good-bye*
> *I remember our faded love*

It was springtime in the Osage. Bob thought back to that first day he arrived to interview Burns. It was the same time of year, two years removed. He wondered if the quail would be on parade in the morning. No lights were on at the house but he could hear voices — and the creak, creak, creaking of rocking chairs.

"Well, the prodigal returns. Come on up here, Bob. We've been saving you a rocker."

There was no mistaking Burns's voice. But who was that with him?

"Hello, Bob."

"Is that you, J.F.?"

"In the flesh."

The three of them shook hands and Bob pulled up a rocker to join them.

"J.F. and I were just reminiscing a bit, Bob. That's what you do when you get old. You sit in a rocker and talk about days gone by."

Bob thought about the old cowboy on the Saturday Evening Post cover — *Dreams of Long Ago*. That was *not* a picture of Burns or J.F.

"I'm not worried about you two. There won't be any grass growing under your feet. My guess is that you're up here hatching out some new scheme."

"Could be, Bob, could be. Listen in. We might need somebody to write a book about it."

"Let me rest a little bit. The last one just about wore me out."

"Shoot, you had the easy part of the deal, Bob. We had to birth the baby and raise it. You just had to write about it."

"I didn't expect to find you up here, J.F. But I'm glad I caught you."

"It's good to see you too, Bob. I guess we missed each other in all of the commotion today. Did you have something on your mind?"

"Yessir, I did. That day I interviewed you two years ago. It was right after I did the Cowboy Boot Camp."

"I remember it well."

"You asked me if I had discovered my purpose."

"And *you* said you hadn't."

"And *you* said it'd come to me."

"And did it?"

"I struggled with it for a long time. I worked my way through your book, which was like a Cowboy Boot Camp booster shot, but I was still at a loss."

J.F. laughed. "You're just trying to make me feel good aren't you?"

"No. That's not what I meant. It was just that my mind was locked on to writing this book and getting it finished. So, I just poured myself into that. And one day as I was feverishly writing away I had an epiphany."

"An epiphany?" Burns stopped rocking. "Listen to this boy, J.F. He had an *epiphany!*" They both laughed.

"Are you guys going to let me get this out or should I just hit the hay?"

"Now he's using words we can understand, Burns. Go ahead, Bob. You know we love you."

"Uh-huh. As I was saying... I had ... uh ... it just hit me one day as I was writing. I was writing about you, Burns... about how you always told a story to make your point. And I had a flashback to that morning when I was sitting here on the porch with you. Do you remember what we talked about?"

"Boy, we covered a lot of ground that day, Bob. I remembered we talked about the power of the Western story but I don't remember everything I said."

"Yes, we talked about Westerns, but it was something *I said* that came back to me. I recorded all of our conversations. I was listening to what we talked about that morning and pulling some quotes from you. That's when I heard it. I said, and I quote, '... as I've listened to your story I've — it's hard to explain — I've thought about *my story*.'"

"I remember you saying something along those lines."

"Well, I got to thinking about that. You said that we have pictures stored in our schemas and that stories allow us to connect with each other because — I know I'm not saying this exactly as you did..."

Burns jumped in to finish what Bob was having trouble saying. "Stories let us see the same pictures in our minds — something like that, right?"

"Pretty much. Then I picked up J.F.'s book and started rereading it. And everything just came together."

J.F. leaned forward. "Tell us about it."

"J.F., your book is basically the story of what you learned on the path of finding and fulfilling your purpose. That provokes readers to think about *their* stories. The exercises force readers to examine their stories until they find what they're seeking. I went back and listened to our interview again. The last thing you told me when I left you that day was, 'Remember, Bob. Your purpose isn't something you define — it's something you *find*. You already possess it — you just haven't found it yet.'

"It occurred to me that my purpose revolved around telling people's stories. And the stories I write impact the lives of the people who read them. *My purpose is to tell stories that positively impact people's lives.*"

"J.F.," Burns started rocking again, "I think Bob here has had an epiphany."

"I think you're right."

"And another thing, Burns," Bob was on a roll now, "I don't agree with you or Thomas Wolfe."

"Where did that come from?"

"You said you can't go home again."

"Whoa, now. Before you get too worked up here, I believe I said you can go home but that home won't be the same. It will have changed. It won't be the same home you left. And I think I also said that you'll always have the memories. And what provoked you to bring all this up anyway? It couldn't have been that *romantic interlude* between you and Sandy on the dance floor tonight could it?" Burns and J.F. looked at each other like two cats that just shared the same canary.

Bob just shook his head. "A guy can't get by with anything around here can he? I didn't see you two at the dance."

"How could you?" J.F. interjected. "Your eyes were closed!"

"You two looked like Fred Astaire and Ginger Rogers," added Burns.

"Who?"

"Oh, never mind, you don't have a picture for them in *your* schema."

"You're just a couple of dirty old men."

After the snickering died down there was a long silence — except for the creaking of the rockers and the music in the distance.

Finally Burns spoke up.

"Bob, the Osage is a good place to live for someone whose purpose is to tell stories that positively impact people's lives. You couldn't find a better place for inspiration. *Just listen.*"

The dance was winding down and the night air carried the not so faraway strains of the song Bobby never tired of hearing.

Many months have come and gone
Since I wandered from my home
In those Oklahoma Hills where I was born
Many a page of life has turned
Many a lesson I have learned
Yet I feel like in those hills I still belong

The youngster never tired of his grandpa's singing but as the night wore on, his eyelids grew heavy and he drifted into the place of his dreams — a place where time stood still and cowboys and Indians forever rode the Oklahoma Hills. And he was right there with them...

> *'Way down yonder in the Indian nation*
> *I rode my pony on the reservation*
> *In the Oklahoma Hills where I was born*
> *'Way down yonder in the Indian nation*
> *A cowboy's life is my occupation*
> *In the Oklahoma Hills where I born*

About the Author

A native Oklahoman, Jim Whitt grew up working on ranches, farms and feedlots. After graduating from Oklahoma State University with a degree in animal science, he became a top producing salesman and marketing executive with two Fortune 500 companies. Jim's purpose-based philosophy was birthed when he discovered his purpose in life: "To help people reach their full potential." That discovery led to the founding of Whitt Enterprises LLC, a firm that helps people and organizations reach their full potential and The Institute for Purposeful Living, a nonprofit organization that helps people find and fulfill their purpose in life.

You can learn more about Jim's speaking and consulting at:

www.ridingforthebrand com

1-800-874-4928